TIME AND TIMELESSNESS IN VIRGINIA WOOLF

Jill Morris

An Exposition-University Book

EXPOSITION PRESS HICKSVILLE, NEW YORK

FIRST EDITION

Library of Congress Catalog Card Number: 77-71590

ISBN 0-682-48805-4

Printed in the United States of America

CONTENTS

TIME AND TIMELESSNESS IN VIRGINIA WOOLF

1

INTRODUCTION

Virginia Woolf took her life in March, 1941. Her fear that she would no longer be able to live meaningfully, according to her ideals and particular vision of life, forced her to choose death as salvation. She joined the flowing waters of the Ouse River, leaving her hat and walking stick on the bank to mark the spot where she parted from a temporal world of fragments, inconsistencies, and isolation, and merged with the ebb and tide of eternal life.

To her, death was not an ending. The spirit above all had to be preserved. Yet in a world where sickness destroys, and wars induce terror and rob one of freedom, the spirit cannot live. Like her character Septimus Warren Smith, under the strain of mental illness, she threw her life away in an act of defiance to preserve that which was most sacred to her—the life and integrity of the soul.

To destroy one's life in an effort to save it seems a contradiction, at least on the surface. There are many such paradoxes in Virginia Woolf's thinking, due, in part, to her emotional makeup, in part to her special way of looking at life and reality.

What is reality? That was the question that preoccupied the author in her work. Each of her novels is an attempt to explore this theme. She also was an experimentalist in technique, for as she became more aware of her vision of life, she attempted to find the most satisfactory form of expressing it. Therefore, she probed not only into life's meaning, but into artistic methods as well. She soon discovered that form and content in a work of art cannot exist separately. An examination of her novels reveals the writer's process; we note a gradual deepening of convictions together with artistic growth, while form and content, which were barely related in her early novels, become inseparable as she realized her creative goals.

Reality—what is it? Is it something tangible, something logical? Is it manifested in society's rules and conventions? Can we grasp it easily, understand it completely? To comprehend reality, as Virginia Woolf envisioned it, we must forget for a moment our surroundings and the age we live in. Let us imagine that we are close to some natural setting, like the ocean. Here, let us compare reality to this vast ocean and individual human lives to the separate waves of that ocean. The waves emerge from the sea; their outlines change as they progress in motion and in external time, and they break on the shore and are pulled back by the tide into ever-moving waters. To Virginia Woolf, reality was Bergson's concept of *durée*—the flowing of life that never subsists; birth, growth, death, the changing of the seasons progress in an unceasing, mechanical rhythm. One human life is but a part of this greater pattern, this reality. Like the waves of the ocean, individual lives are not independent entities, for, like the waves, rising from the sea, they emerge from the wellspring of eternal life only to return at death. In *A Writer's Diary* (September 10, 1928), Virginia Woolf writes that reality is ". . . a thing I see before me: something abstract; but residing in the downs or sky; besides which nothing matters; in which I shall rest and continue to exist. Reality I call it. And I fancy sometimes this is the most necessary thing to me: that which I seek."

In this vision of life as *durée*, the man-invented concepts of time and space have no meaning, for reality exists outside of them. Man, with his temporal life span, views all things in relation to himself and his life on earth. To think in terms other than life beginning when he is born and ending when he dies is difficult, and he consequently organizes his experience into the purely relative formulations of time and space. But reality, as viewed by Virginia Woolf, includes the whole expanse of space and time, and in the ever-flowing stream of life, every living form carries with it a historic and prehistoric past. The present moment is never isolated; it is comprised of every preceding moment, and is constantly in the process of change. Time flows with the stream, having no beginning nor end. Reality, because it contains all space and all time, is actually timeless and spaceless. As T. S. Eliot in "Burnt Norton" writes:*

> *Time present and time past*
> *Are both perhaps present in time future,*
> *And time future contained in time past.*
> *If all time is eternally present*
> *All time is unredeemable.*

Because man is incapable of seeing the whole unity from beginning to end, his view of life is conveniently limited. Mendilow in *Time and the Novel* points out that man's intellect halts the endlessly flowing stream of life at various points and fixes it into forms—"congeals the living flow of reality into a congeries of discontinuous acts."[1]

Virginia Woolf accepted the need, not the validity, of the intellect to arrange life into an understandable pattern—since she, herself, was searching for a pattern. She also realized that the temporal nature of man's life was an obstacle to his grasping the whole of reality. But she knew that in accepting the

---

*From "Burnt Norton" in *Four Quartets*, copyright, 1943, by T. S. Eliot; copyright, 1971, by Esme Valerie Eliot. Reprinted by permission of Harcourt Brace Jovanovich, Inc.

idea that there is an overall pattern to which we, as all living things, belong, she could then grasp fragments of the truth by intuition. Feeling herself a part of something much greater than this person Virginia Woolf—a self which is insignificant by comparison—she would be able to lose her sense of identity (the first step in this mystical type of experience) and merge momentarily with the reality. Clarissa Dalloway (in *Mrs. Dalloway*) walks down Bond Street one summer morning and wonders what will be her relation to this street and others she has traversed when she is dead. She reflects

> that somehow in the streets of London, on the ebb and flow of things, here, there, she survived, Peter survived, lived in each other, she being part, she was positive of the trees at home; of the house there, ugly, rambling all to bits and pieces as it was; part of people she had never met. . . .

Virginia Woolf in her novels repeatedly sets the individual life against human life in perpetual change while the indifferent clock of time ticks away the life of this individual. It was Virginia Woolf's belief that only by being aware of our inner lives—our feelings and sensations, by realizing the flow of our consciousnesses—could we find meaning and comprehend the stream of ever-flowing life, and could we then know that clock time is unreal. Because we as humans are only capable of grasping but moments of reality, Virginia Woolf tried in her novels "to catch the moment, to understand its significance, its ecstasy, and slowly to distill its essence. . . ."[2] In a moment of this sort, the limitations of time and space would be transcended.

To reach the level of our minds where we are at one with our innermost selves involves a cutting off from human society. Reflection, meditation, and truthful recognition of feeling necessitate solitude. But solitude too was painful; silence and solitude were "the worst torture . . . that human beings can inflict," reflects North in her later book, *The Years.* Virginia Woolf believed there was much to be desired in human relationships; communication between people was almost impossible. "We're all afraid of each other," thinks North. Virginia Woolf's characters never say what they want to say. They are sad, alone, and separate. Communication was further hindered because of a person's inability to put into words or action the "myriad of impressions" that filled the consciousness at any instant in time.

Reality, as Virginia Woolf saw it, also demanded a revolution in literary technique and subject matter. Believing in *durée,* one could not at the same time hold to the traditional ideas of novel writing. Personality, language, and plot and structure all had to be considered in a new light: Personality was continuously in the process of taking shape and could not be accomplished by external descriptions; language had to convey the sensations and perceptions of varying levels of awareness all at the same moment, revealing the unconscious as well as the conscious; since action held no interest, plot had to be eliminated. The only thing that mattered was the inner life. In this famous passage from her essay "Modern Fiction" Virginia Woolf sets forth the *raison d'être* of her writing:

> Look within and life, it seems, is very far from being 'like this.' Examine for a moment an ordinary mind on an ordinary day. The mind receives a myriad of impressions—trivial, fantastic, evanescent, or engraved with the sharpness of steel. From all sides they come, an incessant shower of innumerable atoms; and as they fall, as they shape themselves into the

> life of Monday or Tuesday, their accent falls differently from of old; the moment of importance came not here but there; so that, if a writer were a free man and not a slave, if he could write what he chose, not what he must, if he could base his work upon his own feeling, and not upon convention, there would be no plot, no comedy, no tragedy, no love interest or catastrophe in the accepted style, and perhaps not a single button sewn on as the Bond Street tailors would have it. Life is not a series of gig lamps symmetrically arranged; life is a luminous halo, a semi-transparent envelope surrounding us from the beginning of consciousness to the end. Is it not the task of the novelist to convey this varying, this unknown and uncircumscribed spirit, whatever aberration or complexity it may display, with as little mixture of the alien and external as possible? We are not pleading merely for courage and sincerity; we are suggesting that the proper stuff of fiction is a little other than custom would have us believe it. . . . Let us record the atoms as they fall upon the mind in the order in which they fall, let us trace the pattern, however disconnected and incoherent in appearance, which each sight or incident scores upon the consciousness. Let us not take it for granted that life exists more fully in what is commonly thought big than what is commonly thought small.

In Virginia Woolf's handling of time lies a key not only to her mysticism, but to her literary technique. The life of the mind in which psychological time exists is freely moving, untamed, and defiant to conscious will; to create its atmosphere Virginia Woolf had to find a boundary—a frame within which she could allow the inner life to flow freely in any direction and at any pace or intensity. She had to control what seemed uncontrollable. And paradoxically, she did so by using time—fictional time (synonymous with chronological and external time) as one of her major devices. Thus, for example, as one of her characters recalls a moment from the past and loses himself in thoughts and meditations of that moment, a clock strikes (fictional time) and brings him back, often with ruthless severity, to the present. This wish of hers to convey consciousness and eliminate action resulted in a "narrowing of the fictional duration covered by the novel at the same time as the expansion of the psychological duration of the characters. . . ."[3] In some of her work, the writer attempted to give the illusion of all life in one day, of all life in a moment.

Thus Virginia Woolf replaced the outlines of the well-made novel with frames of a temporal or spatial nature and within these frames the inner life, receiving its only direction from the underlying emotional structure, was given full swing. Virginia Woolf did a most unusual thing. She transformed man's misconception of reality into an artistic device in order to make a statement. The man-made concepts of time and space, invented to satisfy a need for some kind of pattern in an otherwise incomprehensible world, became for Virginia Woolf the way to satisfy a need for order in her novels. Her novels, in this sense, were truthful imitations of life as man conceived of it, expressing both an inability to escape completely from the tickings of the chronological clock and also successful flights into the inner reality and timelessness. But although the author thought of reality as consisting of the inner life of the mind and the cyclical rhythms of the universe, she never attempted to deny the existence or even the necessity of man's outer systems; by reality she was referring to the true meaningful life.

Virginia Woolf achieved her personal need for order and

pattern in life in essentially two ways. The first was through her work, which, to be esthetically and emotionally valid, demanded, as does any work of art, a certain wholeness and completion. The second, of course, was through her special vision of reality in which there was an overall pattern in the never-ceasing changing of the seasons, the continual renewal of life, and the ebb and flow of the sea. This latter pattern was only possible to perceive on those rare occasions when intuition pierced the reality. But in death, unity with the universal order was permanent. By choosing to identify with a fixed reality that would not change, she was able to feel herself part of everlasting life, or immortality. The belongingness she thus established was something much more permanent than society or earthly life had to offer. And when she took her own life, merging with the unceasing river, she secured an eternal bond between herself and reality.

To convey consciousness and its multiplicity she used montage—the tricks of the cinema. Some of the devices were slow-ups, fade-outs, cutting, close-ups, panorama, and flashbacks. Through these techniques she was able not only to create the effect of a "flow of events," but also an interrelation or association of ideas, multiplicity, and the infinite expansion of the moment.[4] A device she frequently used in her novels to relate people, not within proximity of one another, at the same instant, and thus suggest an interrelation of ideas, was the striking of a clock; the chimes could be heard for some distance.

And now to begin at the beginning, taking the novels in chronological order and analyzing time both as Virginia Woolf expressed it through the consciousnesses of her characters and through her structural techniques. Time was the key to both her mysticism and also a major literary device—as she struggled to answer such questions as "What does it all mean?" "What is it all about?"

2

THE PRE-EXPERIMENTAL PERIOD

Virginia Woolf's first two novels were pre-experimental; not until she had completed them did she realize that her subject matter required a drastic change in formal expression. She employed in these first books the traditional form of the well-made novel. But in *Monday and Tuesday*, a group of sketches that followed, she left the worn path of nineteenth-century fiction writing to find her own way. These sketches were exercises in subjectivity, close in method to stream of consciousness; plot and action were left with the traditionalists. The new technique was adapted from then on to novel writing, and each succeeding work became an experiment in form and technique. Virginia Woolf was not alone in her search. There were others such as James Joyce who rewrote his already published *Stephen Dedalus* into the stream of consciousness classic, *Portrait of the Artist as a Young Man*.

Virginia Woolf's first books were nevertheless important, since they contained the seeds of the author's evolving technique and conception of reality; in fact, her feelings about death and its relation to reality are nowhere more explicit. And time as a philosophical problem and a structural device played its part—though a minor one. Looking at the formal aspects of *The Voyage Out* and *Night and Day*, we see the author fluctuating between outer description and inner reflection. Which was more important: the world of external events or the inner thought processes? We are not clear, yet the author does drift closer toward the interior life as the novel progresses. Observations and conversations often seem arbitrary and many of the characters, which are superficially rendered, seem merely instruments to reflect the political, moral, and social attitudes of the day from an upper middle-class point of view. A narrator is sometimes on hand to explain feelings and also to indicate the passing of time.

The author uses a form that depends upon the sequence of events for meaning. There is almost no action at all in the plot, because Virginia Woolf has attempted to use plot as a means of revealing aspects of human consciousness and experience.[1] To further complicate matters, she attempts to reveal consciousness in the following ways: attacking facts by irony, meditation, introspection, or delicately shifting dialogue.[2]

If we were to consider the content of the novels, we would know that it was the inner world that concerned Virginia Woolf. Her convictions about reality had already formed before the writing of these books, and she was attempting to express her vision; but her philosophical maturity far exceeded her artistic instrument.

The heroine of *The Voyage Out* is twenty-four-year-old Rachel Vinrace, naive, sheltered, and surprisingly shy and immature for her years, who leaves her uneventful home in London to journey to the Amazon. Both on board ship and in South America, she is exposed to new people, such as the worldly Dalloways, the intellectual St. John Hirst, and the writer Terence Hewet, and to stimulating ideas that awaken her latent potentialities. Rachel begins to grow from a stammering, withdrawn girl to a young woman interested in life;

it is her voyage out—her journey into life, love, and eventually death and reality. The sea is symbolic of the unconscious, the life inside as she struggles toward it.

Rachel's adventure is truly launched when Richard Dalloway embraces her, sending her into tremors of excitement, then terror. That evening she dreams of being trapped in a vault with a gnomish man. It is significant that similar images of horror recur while she is dying, and, as the above, seem to bear no relation to the story. Rachel has never been kissed; love (or is it sex) frightens her. The climax of the story is Rachel's falling in love with Terence. But immediately after they vow their love for each other, Rachel develops a fatal disease; and death unites her forever with reality. Why, one might ask, does the author choose to end the bliss with such finality? In this very first book, we find a theme that recurs in her later books.

The Voyage Out is primarily a search into life's meaning —and also life's lack of meaning which takes the form of lack of communication. "How little we communicate!" Richard Dalloway, a speaker in Parliament, says to Rachel. "This reticence—this isolation—that's what's the matter with modern life." Rachel observes:

> To feel strongly was to create an abyss between oneself and others who feel strongly perhaps but differently. . . .

And later:

> It appeared that nobody ever said a thing they meant, or ever talked of a feeling they felt. . . . Reality dwelling in what one saw and felt, but did not talk about. . .

Partings, separations interrupt the unity that is so desperately sought. When the Dalloways reach their destination and leave the others, Mrs. Dalloway reflects:

> That's the tragedy of life—as I always say!
> Beginning things and having to end them. . . .

Perhaps the most revealing passage is this one, describing the feeling of separation right in the midst of love:

> [Terence and Rachel] remained uncomfortably apart;
> drawn so close together, as she [Rachel] spoke,
> that there seemed no division between them, and
> the next moment separate and far away again. . . .

Terence, who only wishes to be close to Rachel, senses a distance in her. And Rachel, herself, though she loves Terence, acknowledges in her thoughts: ". . . she wanted many more things than the love of one human being—the sea, the sky." She longs to be flung out to sea and washed about the "roots of the world." In envisioning their future together, she reflects that life with Terence would be

> superficial, and had nothing to do with the life that
> went on beneath the eyes and the mouth and the chin,
> for that life was independent of her, and independent
> of everything else.

Although Terence is necessary to Rachel, his love is a trigger to the deeper reality. Her death seems almost a wish on her part.

In death there is even a stronger bond between the lovers. Death in one sense inflicts separation; in another, obliterates it. Rachel dies with her hand in Terence's, and he muses:

> So much the better—this was death. It was nothing; it was to cease to breathe. It was happiness, it was perfect happiness. They had now what they had always wanted to have, the union which had been impossible while they lived.

He is perfectly happy, perfectly fulfilled for that moment until it dawns upon him that he will never see Rachel again. And he cries out, "Rachel! Rachel!" This ambivalence about death demonstrates that death is desirable to the one who dies, devastating to the one who is left. I would venture that a desire not to feel pain is behind each character's easy acceptance of death. Earlier, Terence, finding the knowledge of Rachel's illness (and thereby separation) unbearable, escapes:

> He seemed to stand in an unvexed space of air, on a little island by himself; he was free and immune from pain. It did not matter whether Rachel was well or ill; it did not matter whether they were apart or together; nothing mattered . . . nothing mattered. The waves beat on the shore far away, and the soft wind passed through the branches of the trees, seeming to encircle him with peace and security, with dark and nothingness. Surely the world of strife and fret and anxiety was not the real world, but this was the real world, the world that lay beneath the superficial world, so that, whatever happened, one was secure. . . .

Terence is driven away from the temporal world by too much pain; he achieves a non-anxiety state, a detachment in which he can be at peace. He is making a plea for a world without pain—but, as Virginia Woolf knows, there is no such thing.

On the other hand, we can look at Terence's insight as a momentary penetration of reality wherein his individual wave joins the eternal sea of immortality.

In this depiction of Rachel's illness and impending death, there is suspense; we feel moved, sad. Virginia Woolf in this first novel is capable of evoking emotion—but by eliminating plot and action in the novels that follow *Monday and Tuesday*, she also eliminates passion. They are intriguing, reflective, contemplative, mystical, and contain a quiet, poetic beauty—but we cannot truly say that our emotions are aroused. And in the later novels, death is a running motif—but it is not Terence's anguish; it is death without pain, death with acceptance. Death appears without cause, as part of the continuing stream of life.

The image of waves beating on the shore far away, introduced for the first time in this novel, reappears in all of Virginia Woolf's books to thrust the reader into reality. It is a throbbing reality against which the world of outer events and society are reduced to small significance. Virginia Woolf's reality reaches its pinnacle in *The Waves*, a succession of interior monologues presenting the world of the inner life; so unimportant have external things become that they hardly exist in this novel at all. And in the book that follows, *The Years*, attention curiously shifts to the world of manners and society, focusing upon the meaninglessness of outer events.

In Rachel's death, Virginia Woolf conveys the feeling that life without her goes on very much the same as before. For death, marking the end of an individual's physical existence on earth, is but part of the moving *durée*. In this view of life as an endless stream, death and misfortune lose their intensity and there is no such thing as tragedy. The book ends on the symbolic note of St. John Hirst dozing off:

> Across his eyes passed a procession of objects, black and indistinct, the figures of people picking up their work-baskets, and passing him one after another on their way to bed.

But do not forget that Terence never reappears after his painful separation from Rachel, making his absence noticeably tragic. It is as if he has disappeared too. So, on the one hand, we have the acceptance of death; on the other, the agony.

Aware at this time of her wish to unfold the life of the mind, Virginia Woolf already begins to employ a structural technique she is to develop in her later works. She unites her characters spatially to intensify personality; she isolates her characters on the *Euphrosyne* as they journey across the ocean, and later separates them from the rest of humanity on the small British colony in South America throughout the remainder of the book.

She is also aware of time, the evocation of the past, as a device to add dimension to the present moment. Terence Hewet, writer and mouthpiece for the author, tells Rachel about the book he hopes to write (a book about silence incidentally):

> My idea is that there's a certain quality of beauty in the past, which the ordinary historical novelist completely ruins by his absurd conventions. The moon becomes the Regent of the Skies. People clap spurs to their horses, and so on. I'm going to treat people as though they were exactly the same as we are. The advantage is that, detached from modern conditions, one can make them more intense and more abstract than people who live as we do.

There are many references to the past in this novel. Rachel during her voyage out reads Gibbon's *History of the Roman Empire*, which feels to her like taking "roads back to the very beginning of the world." Time appears to move both forward and backward simultaneously.

Virginia Woolf escapes "from the tyranny of the time sequence" through the device of Helen Ambrose's embroidery, as J. K. Johnstone points out.[3] Mrs. Ambrose is working over some embroidery which depicts a tropical river. It is at a tropical river that Rachel contracts at a later date the illness leading to her death. Virginia Woolf describes Helen in this situation as a fate, outside the limits of time and space, for as she embroidered, her "figure possessed the sublimity of a woman's of the early world, spinning the thread of fate." Through this device, Johnstone explains, the author slows down the stream of time and unites the present with the future. Mrs. Ambrose and her embroidery are symbolic of the pattern behind everything, the rhythmic continuity of life that is everlasting, unaffected by the events of the temporal world. The act of sewing itself is a rhythmic act, which Virginia Woolf repeats in later novels to create the feeling of the "reality"—the ebb and flow of the sea, the change of the seasons.

And early in the book, Rachel meditates upon a line from *Tristan* that refers to a "corpse-like Bride." Almost immediately she remembers her mother's funeral. In this image of death, past and future merge and we have a prognostication of Rachel's fate.

Night and Day, Virginia Woolf's second novel, in which there is again confusion in execution, is on the surface a traditional novel, but underneath is an attempt to reveal the inner lives and mental reactions of the characters to experience. The author tries to force her conceptions about the human personality and its behavior into objective patterns (separation, reunion, falling in or out of love), devices which "are arbitrarily and not necessarily connected with the flow of ideas and mental responses which constitute the novel's main interest."[4] Not only is the meaning of the book at times confused but the style is poor, endlessly jumping, and lacking smooth transition, from action to reflection. Virginia Woolf does succeed in exposing the mind, but she is not yet inside it.

The four main characters are Mary Datchet, Ralph Denham, Katherine Hilberry, and William Rodney—people confused about love and the conflict between sharing oneself with another and the opposing need for isolation and independence (which Virginia Woolf correlates with freedom). The meaning of the book lies in their progression from confusion to understanding; it is their "voyage out." Katherine considers the major conflict, implicit in the title of the book:

> Why, she reflected, should there be this perpetual disparity between the thought and the action, between the life of solitude and the life of society, this astonishing precipice on one side of which the soul was active and in broad daylight, on the other side of which it was contemplative and dark as night? Was it not possible to step from one to the other, erect, and without essential change?

The novel ends on a note of happiness (although we cannot be assured of its permanence); Ralph and Katherine feel both secure in their love for each other and also free to pursue the interests of their separate worlds. It is an idealistic love relationship wherein one partner need not submit to the will of the other. Love and freedom coexist.

Night and Day, as does her first book, has significant moments when life's pattern is clearly seen. For example, as Katherine walks down Kingsway, a busy commercial street, swarming with pedestrians, she thinks about

> the inexpressible fascination of varied life pouring ceaselessly with a purpose which, as she looked, seemed to her, somehow, the normal purpose for which life was framed; its complete indifference to the individuals, whom it swallowed up and rolled onwards, filled her with at least a temporary exaltation. . . .

Ambiguity is clearly contained in this reflection, since it is this very "indifference to the individuals" that makes reality, as most of us view it, intolerable, and for which Virginia Woolf had to find an explanation. Rather than rebel futilely against time's ineluctable consumption of life, it would seem that she submitted to time's indifference by thinking of it in abstract terms; in her new reality, she mentally shattered the existence of chronological time and of death.

Virginia Woolf's concern with the question of time in *Night and Day* is expressed even in the title of the book. The theme of time-gone-by comes through in the Hilberry house with all its reminders of the past—the portrait of Ruskin, for example, whom Katherine's mother compares to Denham, thereby establishing a connection between past and present. At the very beginning of the book, Mrs. Hilberry says:

> After all, what is the present? Half of it's the past and the better half, too, I should say.

And as Mary Datchet sits performing the symbolic act of knitting, she thinks about her life:

> As she ran needles in and out of the wool, she thought of the various stages in her own life which made her present position seem the culmination of successive miracles.

Time, after the termination of this novel, begins to take on a new structural importance.

3

JACOB'S ROOM

At first glance, one could hardly believe that *Jacob's Room* was written by the same author as *The Voyage Out* and *Night and Day*, so different is it from these novels in technique. But Virginia Woolf, having had a chance to experiment with her art—producing *Monday and Tuesday*, a series of sketches that approached the new stream of consciousness technique—discovered a method more effective than before for expressing her unique vision of life. With this method, she placed the same importance upon form and structure as does the poet in enhancing his meanings. Yet *Jacob's Room*, although a step in the right direction, reflects the uncertainty of change—like the adolescent who runs from home in his struggle for selfhood and independence only to scurry back to childhood security when his new freedom and its added responsibility demand too much. *Jacob's Room* cannot stand on its own and directly speak for itself; there is still a narrator on hand to describe events and to convey the author's thoughts about literature and human nature. And the appearance of this narrator is one of the things that weakens the structure of Mrs. Woolf's book.

Before analyzing the structure, it would be best to briefly describe the content of *Jacob's Room*. We see it, on the surface, as a biography of a young man named Jacob, representative of a class of fairly well-to-do Englishmen who grow up, go to Cambridge, fall in love, and travel. (He is the male counterpart of Rachel.) In reality, the book is not so much a study of Jacob as it is the author's impression of life as it flows in and around her central character. This is perhaps why the book is called *Jacob's Room* rather than just plain *Jacob,* because his room is the life surrounding him wherever he is—be it the beach in Cornwall as a child, Scarborough during his boyhood days, the University at Cambridge—or London, Paris, Greece, or Italy. At the end of the book we know little about Jacob, but we do know a lot about Virginia Woolf and how *she* feels about life. Jacob is too closely linked with his environment to be ever distinguished as an individual. Yet he is necessary to the unity of the book. Jacob is the eye through which we see, "the thread, which holds together in a unity her [the author's] series of visions, revelations, etc., . . . the bright fragments [are] the author's sense of life—not Jacob's life, but the life in which Jacob moves."[1]

When we complete the book, we feel that hardly anything has happened. Even his death seems inconsequential, which is perhaps the author's intention. Just before we learn of his demise, we view Jacob for the last time from the eyes of people who see him on the street—a technique to bring him boldly up to the present moment. Jacob isn't even there to witness his own death. Only in the last page of the novel, do we learn that he has died. There has been no hint of it, only a premonition; Jacob's mother, standing in his room, holds up his old shoes and says, "What am I to do with these?" Several pages before, she hears in present-day London the sound of guns emanating from ancient Greece, symbolically announcing Jacob's untimely end:

> . . . the ships in Piraeus fired their guns. . . .
> Darkness drops like a knife over Greece. "Not at this distance," she thought. "It's the sea." Again, far

> away, she heard the full sound, as if nocturnal women were beating great carpets. There was Morty lost, and Seabrook dead; her sons fighting for their country.

Events such as Jacob's death seem trivial not merely because Jacob has never really lived as a character, but also because of the way in which time is handled. Notice in the above passage how the past takes precedence over the present, and how the present seems relatively unimportant. The blast of guns in one throbbing moment tells the death of thousands of young men who have died through the centuries defending their country. What is one Jacob when we think of the number who had died like him!

The hero of the book exists now only in the memory of those who have known him, symbolized in the story by his mother's and friend's return to his empty room. The book ends and we are left with the feeling of having traveled to many places, of having seen life vividly at moments—though we have caught only glimpses of Jacob's life, and those mainly through the eyes of other people. This is Jacob's voyage out. Like Rachel, he falls in love, then dies suddenly.

The glimpses and episodes we have witnessed are each significant in themselves, but bear little relation to each other, nor do they add up to an overall meaning. Because this novel is basically impressionistic, unity would have to depend upon some underlying emotional structure to tie the separate parts together, according to critic David Daiches. But Jacob is not a strong enough unifying device. And although the episodes are linked to one another, the relations between them and the transitions between characters are "arbitrary . . . determined not by any preconceived scale of emphasis but by the needs of the moment—the need for indicating the interrelationship of different experiences. . . ."[2] Although Virginia Woolf has attempted to present a whole, she has succeeded in fragmentariness—the fragmentariness which tormented her so in life—rather than unity.

Lack of unity is actually the greatest weakness of the book. But we wonder whether Virginia Woolf truly intended to shape Jacob into a living, flesh-and-blood character at all or whether her purpose was primarily to present her overall view of life—and her vision of reality. The past, you might say, was more the hero of this book than Jacob himself, who served largely as a vehicle through which the past could speak. For example, Jacob's death—as has already been pointed out—echoes similar deaths of young men in ancient Greece who were killed in war. The present event's significance is in its reflection of the past. The setting, twentieth-century Athens, carries with it a significant history. And when, at the very end of the book, Mrs. Flanders holds up Jacob's baby shoes, we feel less the loss of Jacob and more the idea behind the symbolism of this action—that life is everlasting and shall continue long after Jacob or, in fact, any other character in the novel, including Topaz the cat.

With the fragments all added up together, we have a structure that is episodic; events usually follow each other in chronological order as Virginia Woolf traces her main character from early childhood to young manhood. Often several events occur at the same moment, thereby giving the impression of multiplicity and reality.

Time permeates the novel. Her episodes are "brief portions of time and limited segments of space" which are enveloped by eternity and surrounded by all space.[3] By this structure, not only does Virginia Woolf give a sense of the past in every present moment, but she intensifies her scenes—pinpointing a moment in time, a point in space—and lends them depth.

When we see Jacob in Cambridge, for example, pictures of Turkey and the past break through:

> And then before one's eye would come the bare hills of Turkey—sharp lines, dry earth, coloured flowers, and colour on the shoulders of the women, standing naked-legged in the stream to beat linen on the stones. The stream made loops of water round their ankles. But none of that could show clearly through the swaddlings and blanketings of the Cambridge night. The stroke of the clock even was muffled; as if intoned by somebody reverent from a pulpit; as if generations of learned men heard the last hour go rolling through their ranks and issued it, already smooth and time-worn, with their blessing, for the use of the living. Was it to receive this gift from the past that the young man came to the window and stood there, looking out across the court? It was Jacob. He stood smoking his pipe while the last stroke of the clock purred softly round him . . . the sound of the clock conveying to him (it may be) a sense of old buildings and time; and himself the inheritor; and then tomorrow; and friends. . . .

In the quoted passage, the muffled strokes of the Cambridge clock (the most recent vibrations, as they are, from an ancient timepiece) speak of the past's strength and reality behind the present moment.

There are many other instances where the author takes us back through the centuries. In Scarborough, for example, Mrs. Flanders and Mrs. Jarvis are one evening at a Roman camp above town with the nearby church and its dead and the eternal moors in the background. And as we wander back into the past suggested by images of bones and rusty swords, the church clock marks off present time—striking the hours and quarter hours.

Johnstone has noted subtle devices by which Mrs. Woolf sections off portions of present time and space—the emptying of a bag of cherries by Timmy Durrant as he lies nibbling them in a punt at Cambridge, "the steady march of the hours of an evening at sea" accompanying Timmy's and Jacob's cruise around Land's End, the flight of a bumblebee relating in space by its flight people in the garden, and a ship sailing by a window through which Jacob peers and then a light flashing on to mark the end of the pier.[4]

With other devices Virginia Woolf destroys the concept of chronological time, merging past and future in the present moment and roaming freely up and down the stream of time without respect for the sequence of events. But she mentions either the month, the year, the locale, or Jacob's age as devices to give the reader a reference point in the present so that he does not become lost in the stream. In one instance, Mrs. Woolf introduces to her reader the Reverend Mr. Floyd who teaches Latin to young Jacob. Then she steps out of Jacob's boyhood to trace Mr. Floyd's life from his leaving Scarborough to his retiring in Hampstead after a successful career—"often to be seen feeding the ducks on Leg of Mutton Pond." One day Mr. Floyd sees Jacob on the street; Jacob is a young man now. Not until this point do we return to Jacob's boyhood to follow the natural order of events. We return for a second time, near the end of the book, to the meeting already reported between Jacob and Mr. Floyd.

By giving us this glimpse into the future, Virginia Woolf removes any element of suspense that might be present (as in the dramatic novel, for example). We are prematurely prepared to progress to this future moment.

To write about life horizontally, as the author did, obviates the necessity of explaining what has happened. We fill in the gaps with our imaginations. The brief touches about Jimmy and Helen, for instance: before World War I, Jimmy doesn't ask Helen, who loves him, to marry him. Later Mrs. Woolf writes: "And now Jimmy feeds crows in Flanders and Helen visits hospitals." This is life without a bang—a nostalgic, wistful view.

All the techniques mentioned thus far recur in the author's later works. According to one critic, it was these experiments in technique which brought about the failure of unity and overall meaning in *Jacob's Room.* "Virginia Woolf's exploration of time and space . . . often become an end in itself—a search . . . for reality; and there is, in consequence, a division in the book between the particular and the general impressions which it contains. . . . Scenes are seldomly 'well-coordinated' with the realms of space and time which surround them."[5] The exception to this is the three-dimensional, organic opening scene on the Cornish Beach. In her imagery Virginia Woolf paints a beautiful canvas where events are minutely described against the waves of the eternal sea beating upon the shore. This scene is indicative of what will follow in her novels.

Bernard Blackstone excuses Mrs. Woolf's failure to unite the scenes of her novel to form a pattern from which the meaning would evolve, explaining that this fragmentariness is true to life, for when one is young, life is like that.[6] But even if it were Virginia Woolf's intention to write about Jacob's life and the indecisiveness of his youth—which I doubt—fragmentariness in this novel would be a flaw. For if she wished to show fragmentariness in the life of her hero, she was mistaken to repeat it in the structure of her book; a work of art should give the illusion of life, not try to imitate life; and though the life it represents lacks order and apparent meaning, the novel itself must have order and message.

The unity that does exist in *Jacob's Room,* a unity involving a relation between past and present time, is to a degree produced by the author's continuous repetition of images that convey a sense of the past and reality—the sea, the lighthouse, Byron, the moors, the sheep's skull; all of these existed before Jacob and lend the depth of history to the relatively short span of fictional time covered by the novel.

Virginia Woolf has many things to say about time in *Jacob's Room.* For one, the mixture of past and present, life and death, is "exhilarating." Jacob's mother, upon hearing a funeral bell off in the distance, thinks of her dead husband Seabrook. At that instant her son calls to her:

> Sounding at the same moment as the bell,
> her son's voice mixed life and death, inextricably,
> exhilaratingly.

However time is treacherous; we decay:

> There on the sand not far from the lovers lay the
> old sheep's skull without its jaw. Clean, white,
> wind-swept, sand-rubbed. An unpolluted piece
> of bone existed nowhere on the coast of Cornwall.
> The sea holly would grow through the eye-socket;
> it would turn to powder, or some golfer hitting
> his ball one fine day, would disperse a little dust.

But time does not touch those things of immortal beauty:

> . . . far from being decayed, the Parthenon appears, on the contrary, likely to outlast the entire world.

And time does not change the pattern of human life:

> But what century have we reached? Has this procession from the Surrey Side to the Strand gone on forever? That old man has been crossing the bridge these six hundred years. . . . He shuffles on. No one stands still. It seems as if we marched to the sound of music; perhaps the wind and the river; perhaps these same drums and trumpets—the ecstasy and hubbub of the soul.

However—as individuals taking a narrower view of time—can we ever accept without protest the shortening of our lives with each ticking of the clock, or do we feel a sense of panic and meaninglessness at the thought of time moving on and consuming us? Sandra Wentworth Williams—the only woman Jacob has ever loved—looks back upon her life and tells herself that she has had her moments:

> Meanwhile the great clock on the landing ticked and Sandra would hear time accumulating and ask herself, "What for? What for?"

And Clara Durrant, who has loved Jacob, cries, as a horse gallops past:

Oh stop! Stop it, Mr. Bowley!

She has just passed the statue of Achilles, who, like Jacob, was caught by the heel in the prime of life.

It seems that the author has many ideas about time, involving both acceptance and protest, that are not yet resolved in her mind. And she continues to explore these questions in each of her remaining novels, examining the meaning of life and its relation to time and death.

4

MRS. DALLOWAY

Virginia Woolf was called an experimentalist with good reason. In each new novel she attempted to find the form that would give power and beauty to her content. And not only did she strive for new forms, but she was forced by her artistic sensibility and integrity to recognize the flaws of the previous work and correct them. Thus, in *Mrs. Dalloway* she found the way to overcome the fragmentariness and disunity of *Jacob's Room* and at the same time express her attitudes about time and reality. *Mrs. Dalloway* is an achievement in formal and emotional integration.

The book covers one day in June, 1922, in London's West End. The time and the place—these elements together "make the frame for the novel within which, as in a picture, the material exists . . . and becomes a part of the form and therefore of the meaning. This integration is achieved by the novel's inner rhythm, a quality of continuity and flow that picks up each detail, places it where it belongs in the pattern, and moves on to the next without losing contact with what is left behind. . . ."[1]

Time and place (outer world) keep us aware of the position or the physical reality of the characters while the emotional reflective content of their consciousnesses unfolds. Big Ben is as important a character, though in a different sense, as Mrs. Dalloway herself. As Big Ben strikes the hours and quarter hours, his "leaden circles dissolve in the air," uniting time with place and the consciousness of that character who is present.

The characters of the novel are related to one another not only in time and space, but also psychologically and spiritually. For example, when Virginia Woolf suddenly breaks away from Septimus Warren Smith's thoughts and jumps to those of Elizabeth Dalloway, she creates a common bond between these characters—although they do not know each other. On this one day in June, we learn the significant lifetime experiences and precious memories of the central characters as their inner consciousnesses unravel before us. Chronological time (this June day) and psychological time are in a counterpoint relation.

Now to look more closely at the character who does the relating—Big Ben. He is primarily a unifier, but has other functions as well. When Big Ben strikes, those who hear are lifted out of their absorption in daily living to be reminded of *this* moment out of all the rest. There is a heightened awareness of life at this moment when time stands still and past and future merge. "Time gives emphasis."[2] And we can always depend upon Big Ben to speak at the significant moments of the book—for example, when Septimus Warren Smith throws himself from the window, or when Mrs. Dalloway feels the intensity of life and experiences a sense of being far away at sea. Big Ben calls our attention to what is meaningful, such as life and death, questions that form the roots of our natural curiosity. And each time Big Ben strikes and we rise from the daily problems of existence to either struggle with or contemplate the universal questions, Virginia Woolf reminds us of two things—that each individual life is but a part of the all-encompassing stream, and that with every passing moment, our earthly lives are ebbing away from us. How much Virginia Woolf is concerned in this novel with the problems of aging and death! She is without doubt obsessed with death (both attracted to it and frightened by it). No wonder she explored the questions of time and reality so ardently. Although she clung to the idea of merging after death in the stream and reality, a part of her feared intensely the conclusion of life; perhaps her beautifully formulated idea of reality was, in part, based upon this fear. But, to deal with tangibles, let us see how Virginia Woolf achieved organic unity in *Mrs. Dalloway* with Big Ben as her chief device.

The book opens on a glorious Wednesday morning in June; it is postwar England in 1922. Clarissa Dalloway is preparing for the party she is having that evening. From the very start, the reader is given, through the mind of Clarissa, glimpses of the major characters and themes that will develop as the book progresses. Before we meet them in person, we know the characters as Clarissa knows them. The beauty of this day in June reminds Mrs. Dalloway of a similar day in her past when she was a girl of eighteen at Bourton. Bourton keeps returning to her consciousness throughout the day, and gradually there evolves the whole story of her romance with Peter, her attachment to Sally Seton, and her meeting with Richard, her husband, in addition to references to minor characters such as Hugh Whitbread and her aunt. The themes develop when we view them through the consciousness of other characters—for example, Peter, whom we will meet later on and whose thoughts also return to Bourton. The personalities of the important characters are known through the impressions and memories others have of them, and the thoughts and feelings that they have about themselves. Clarissa and the others are presented as they are now and as they were thirty years ago.

But Clarissa's thoughts are directed not only toward her memories of Bourton, but also to present concerns such as: her daughter Elizabeth who is under the influence of Miss Kilman, a tyrannical, miserable, and hypocritical religious fanatic who teaches Elizabeth history and tries to win her affection; feeling both young and aged and far out to sea; life and reality and love; about how she loves London on this day in June; and about her party that evening. The party is the anticipated point in future chronological time, where all the people we shall meet on this day appear, if not physically, then spiritually. The reader moves back in time to Clarissa's girlhood at Bourton and forward to the party that evening. And in external time, the book carries us forward to the very moment of the party, so that we are absorbed in the happenings of this short span of time from ten in the morning to three in the evening, as well as in the events of the past. Each thought, feeling, and response of this day is related to all previous ones; there is no present moment that can be separated from its cumulative past. The movement in the book, as we can see, is produced by the author's handling of time.

There are two concentric circles of activity in *Mrs. Dalloway*, the one having as its core Clarissa with her love of life, and the other, Septimus Warren Smith whose mental suffering forces him to embrace death. "Life and death form the inexhaustible counterpoint of her [Virginia Woolf's] work. Not death coming as the ending to a completed story, but death inexplicable, torturing, making life meaningless; yet also mysterious, fascinating, giving depth to life. From these two strands—a feeling for the richness and beauty of life, and a patient recognition of the sovereignty and cruelty of death—her supreme themes are woven."[3] Though Septimus and Clarissa never meet, they are linked together psychologically, intuitively, in space, and in time, and at the end of the book are united in a spiritual bond. Thus, the two opposing forces—life and death—merge and become part of the eternal stream of life. This relationship between Clarissa and Septimus is the basic design of the book.

The first section opens with Mrs. Dalloway on her way to purchase flowers for the party that evening. As she walks through Westminster, and we follow her thoughts and reflections, we are reminded of her movements in space and her relation to the external world by such practical considerations as waiting on the curb for Durtnall's van to pass. It is these realities which interrupt her reflections and, at the same time, present her both inwardly and outwardly to the reader.

On page five of *Mrs. Dalloway*, Big Ben makes his first appearance in the novel as he strikes the hour. "The leaden circles dissolved in the air." Thus, not only do we hear the sound, but we have a visual picture of it in our imaginations as well.

> Such fools we are, she [Clarissa] thought, crossing Victoria Street. For Heaven only knows why we love it so.

It is as if the clock's striking the hour reminds Clarissa on a subconscious level that time is passing and that this is life, for she reflects on how she loves it so, this "moment" of life. She describes moving humanity, thus giving an illustration of the Bergsonian concept of life's flux:

> In people's eyes, in the swing, tramp, and trudge; in the bellow and the uproar; the carriages, motor cars, omnibuses, vans, sandwich men shuffling and swinging; brass bands; barrel organs; in the triumph and the jingle and the strange high singing of some aeroplane overhead was what she loved; life; London; this moment of June.

From Clarissa's thoughts about life, she gradually shifts to the opposite swing of the emotional pendulum and thinks about death. Death to her is but an aspect of the continual cyclical force, a part of *durée*, and this sets up in a subtle way the relation between Septimus and Clarissa, even though Septimus is not referred to at all in her meditation.

The first section of the book (there are no chapters) closes in the flower shop with Clarissa starting at the sound of what appeared to be a pistol shot in the street. The second section opens in the street where everybody is focusing upon the motor car that has caused the explosion. Thus, in the same instant of time, we jump from Clarissa's consciousness to those of the people outside, and Septimus is among them. The unifying link between characters is not, this time, the chiming of Big Ben, but rather the loud explosion from the motor car. Septimus tries to pass this vehicle that has stopped on the road.

> Everything had come to a standstill. The throb of the motor engines sounded like a pulse irregularly drumming through an entire body. . . .

The stream of life comes to a halt for one moment, and in that stillness the rhythmic throbbing of life is felt.

The reader enters into the consciousnesses of Septimus and Rezia, his wife. Rezia who is thinking about Septimus's recent threat to kill himself suddenly remembers last autumn when they were happy together. All eyes are upon the motor car as it proceeds toward Piccadilly, carrying some royal personage, and serving as a spatial link between characters.

Mrs. Dalloway leaves Mulberry's flower shop, while the crowd gathers at the gates of Buckingham Palace to await the arrival of the royal car. Then suddenly, there is heard the sound of an airplane directly overhead and all eyes turn upward. As their eyes focus upon the plane writing in the sky,

> the whole world became perfectly silent, and a flight of gulls crossed the sky, first one gull leading, then another, and in this extraordinary silence and peace, in this pallor, in this purity, bells struck eleven times, the sound fading up there among the gulls.

In the midst of this serenity, the chiming bells and flight of gulls bring the message that time is passing, yet there is the feeling of eternity behind it.

> Rezia cries to herself that she is alone, as perhaps at midnight, when all boundaries are lost, the country reverts to its ancient shape, as the Romans saw it, lying cloudy, when they landed, and the hills had no names and rivers wound they knew not where—such was her darkness.

This is one of Virginia Woolf's favorite images—one that is to be repeated over and and over again in her succeeding novels. The flight into the past that is symbolized in the above passage is something far beyond Rezia's experience in this life; she is returning to a period when mankind itself was in its embryonic stage.

Section two ends with a description of the skywriting of the airplane. The third section opens with Clarissa Dalloway, who has just arrived at the front steps of her house asking the maid what everybody is looking at. During the time that the reader was in the consciousness of Rezia and was attending to the people looking at the skywriting, Clarissa was walking home from Mulberry's flower shop. Though our attention may be focused elsewhere, we are always aware of the positions of all the main characters in time and space; therefore, a sudden shift into a different consciousness never comes as a shock to us. The novel is similar to a stage in which all the performers are in view; though we may be attending to the soliloquy of one character, his movement, or interaction with others, we are still aware, but to a lesser degree, of the positions and movements of the other people on the stage.

Clarissa, disappointed at not being invited with her husband Richard to Lady Bruton's luncheon party, retreats to her attic room. She goes to her desk:

> The candle was half burned down and she had read deep in Baron Marbot's *Memoirs.*

This is symbolic of Mrs. Dalloway's having reached her middle years of life. She fears that she is getting old and that time is running out. But suddenly, she remembers an ecstatic moment when Sally Seton, the girl whom she so admired, kissed her at Bourton. This was one of those rare moments in which time stood still and there was, for one split second, a meaningful penetration of reality. Now Clarissa meditates:

> She was not old yet. She had just broken into her fifty-second year. Months and months of it were still untouched. June, July, August! Each still remained almost whole, and as if to catch the falling drop, Clarissa (crossing to the dressing-table) plunged into

> the very heart of the moment, transfixed it, there—the moment of this June morning on which was the pressure of all other mornings.

In preparation for the party that night, Clarissa sews the tears in her mermaid-green dress.

> Quiet descended on her, calm, content, as her needle, drawing the silk smoothly to its gentle pause, collected the green folds together and attached them very lightly to the belt. So on a summer's day waves collect, over-balance, and fall; and the whole world seems to be saying "that is all" more and more ponderously, until even the heart in the body which lies in the sun on the beach says too, That is all. Fear no more says the heart. Fear no more, says the heart, committing its burden to some sea, which sighs collectively for all sorrows, and renews, begins, collects, lets fall. And the body alone listens to the passing bee; the waves breaking; the dog barking, far away barking and barking.

This passage is of great importance and becomes even more significant as the book develops. The sea symbolizes timelessness and eternity. The waves are the individual lives that eventually join this all-embracing sea of change. "Fear no more the heat of the sun" is a Shakespearean refrain that reappears in the consciousness of Septimus just before he takes his own life, and establishes that strong relationship between Clarissa and Septimus, whom she does not know—between life and death.

It is the ringing of the front-door bell this time that interrupts Clarissa's thoughts and announces the arrival of Peter, just returned from India. At the sound of the bell, Clarissa's first reaction is to think of the hour; she has returned to the material world of time and space. The doorbell takes over the function of Big Ben by announcing the time and bringing characters into contact with one another. We return once more to the scene at Bourton through the reminiscences of Peter and Clarissa; each time Bourton returns, the reader sees it more vividly. Not only are Clarissa and Peter living the scene in their past, but they are also working out the scene of the present, the now.

Elizabeth enters the room where the two old friends are talking, and

> the sound of Big Ben striking the half-hour struck between them with extraordinary vigour, as if a young man, strong, indifferent, inconsiderate, were swinging dumb-bells this way and that.

The indifferent hands of time progress on and on, incognizant of the two people who had been in love thirty-four years ago. Though they sit in a room together and feel as deeply as they once did, the passage of time cannot be denied. The arrival of Clarissa's daughter, accompanied by the chimes of Big Ben, illustrates this reality.

As Peter makes his exit, Clarissa calls after him: "Remember my party tonight" with the clocks striking the half-hour in the background. The new section begins; the clocks are still striking and Clarissa's words, "Remember my party," resound again and again in Peter's ears as he walks down Victoria Street. It is half-past eleven. Peter thinks about Clarissa, about her coldness and how she has refused him.

> Then, as the sound of St. Margaret's languished, he thought, she has been ill, and the sound expressed languor and suffering. It was her heart, he remembered; and the sudden loudness of the final stroke tolled for death that surprised in the midst of life, Clarissa falling where she stood in her drawing-room. No! No! he cried. She is not dead! I am not old, he cried, and marched up Whitehall, as if there rolled down to him, vigorous, unending, his future.

There is no doubt as to Virginia Woolf's preoccupation with the problems of time passing and the approach of death. The clocks serve to remind her characters that they are getting older and that death is drawing near; they continually try to escape from these thoughts.

We follow Peter into the park where he falls asleep on a bench. The journey to the park takes us right into the lives of Rezia and Septimus, who are within proximity of the dozing Peter. Septimus is having a hallucination; he sees his friend Evans, who was killed in the war, appear from behind a tree. Rezia, not knowing what is going on in his mind, attempts to bring him back to the outside world by asking him, of all things, the time.

> As he sat smiling at the dead man in the grey suit, the quarter struck—the quarter to twelve. . . . And that is being young, Peter Walsh thought as he passed them.

The irony of this thought illustrates how isolated we human beings are from each other. Though there has been no formal introduction nor communication between persons in the ordinary sense, we can say that there now exists some relation between Peter, Septimus and Rezia. Circumstances of time and space have brought them into contact, and they have exchanged thoughts about each other. They have come together for but one instant in time, and now they separate. Peter leaves the park and steps into a taxi; Rezia and Septimus are on their way to see Dr. William Bradshaw, the famous nerve specialist.

The next time that the clocks strike it is noon, and the sound reminds us of the positions of each of the characters upon the stage of this novel.

> It was precisely twelve o'clock; twelve by Big Ben; whose stroke was wafted over the northern part of London; blent with that of other clocks, mixed in a thin ethereal way with the clouds and wisps of smoke, and died up there among the seagulls—twelve o'clock struck as Clarissa Dalloway laid her green dress on her bed, and the Warren Smiths walked down Harley Street. Twelve was the hour of their appointment. Probably, Rezia thought, that was Sir William Bradshaw's house with the grey motor car in front of it. The leaden circles dissolved in the air.

The interview between Sir William Bradshaw and the Septimus Warren Smiths follows. The doctor sees in a glance that there is something seriously wrong with Septimus; he tries to establish communication with him but does not succeed. Septimus suddenly is about to confess something to the doctor that could mark the turning point back to sanity, but the doctor glances at his watch and politely dismisses them. For he gave precisely three-quarters of an hour to each patient. Time plays an important part in the irony of this situation. Perhaps it demonstrates how Virginia Woolf hates it so. And Virginia Woolf, having had her own siege of mental illness, is making a contemptuous statement about psychiatrists.

At half-past one, a commercial clock, suspended above the shop of Messrs. Rigby and Lowndes in Oxford Street, broadcasts the hour. Hugh Whitbread, whom Clarissa had accidentally met for a brief moment on her way from the flowers that morning, looks up at the clock; he is going to Lady Bruton's for lunch. He and Richard Dalloway and Lady Bruton dine together, and when the guests depart, Lady Bruton retires to her room. She thinks about her friends, Richard Dalloway and Hugh Whitbread:

> And they went further and further from her, being attached to her by a thin thread (since they had lunched with her) which would stretch and stretch, get thinner and thinner as they walked across London; as if one's friends were attached to one's body, after lunching with them, by a thin thread, which (as she dozed there) became hazy with the sound of bells, striking the hour or ringing to service, as a single spider's thread is blotted with rain-drops, and, burdened, sags down, So she slept. . . . And Richard Dalloway and Hugh Whitbread hesitated at the corner of Conduit Street at the very moment that Millicent Bruton, lying on the sofa, let the thread snap; snored.

The bells and the imaginary spider's thread, both, serve as the connecting link between characters.

As Richard Dalloway, with flowers in his hand, approaches his front door, wanting to tell Clarissa how he loves her, Big

Ben chimes loudly. The next paragraph begins with a description of the sound of Big Ben flooding Clarissa's drawing room. She shudders at the thought that at this very hour her daughter Elizabeth is at prayer with that horrible woman, Doris Kilman. The clock finishes striking three as Richard enters his wife's drawing room.

Clarissa, after seeing Richard who is now off to a meeting at Parliament, retires to her room for a nap. Big Ben strikes the half-hour as she stares at an old lady in the room opposite, who symbolizes to her privacy of the soul. This is the revelation, the miracle—privacy of the soul; and as Clarissa thinks this, the striking of the clocks makes this moment stand out from all the others.

In contrast to this scene, we now enter the mind of Doris Kilman, who represents to Mrs. Dalloway tyranny and destruction of the soul. The late clock, which sounded two minutes after Big Ben, strikes and it

> seemed to break, like the spray of an exhausted wave, upon the body of Miss Kilman standing still in the street for a moment to mutter, "It is the flesh."

The reader enters both the consciousnesses of Doris Kilman and Elizabeth, at tea together. There ensues a painful scene and when they part, we follow Miss Kilman to the Abbey where she prays and tries to control the flesh. Then we enter into the mind of Elizabeth as she mounts an omnibus and rides up Whitehall. Time passes. An alternation of light and dark is produced by the flight of individual clouds over the sun. This fluctuation of dark and light, symbolic of human emotions and the inner and outer worlds (*Night and Day*), acts as a link between Elizabeth and Septimus Smith who is lying on a sofa in his sitting room watching the light and shadow on the wall. Septimus is having thoughts very like those of Mrs. Dalloway as she was mending the tear in her dress. He pictures himself

> bathing, floating, on the top of the waves, while far away on shore he heard dogs barking and barking far away. Fear no more, says the heart in the body, fear no more.

And not much time elapses before Septimus throws himself from the window, while the clock strikes six, as if tolling for death.

While the ambulance, carrying Septimus's body, whizzes away, Peter Walsh, whose attention has been caught, ironically thinks that this is a remarkable age in which he lives, this age of modern mechanics.

> And yet, thought Peter Walsh, as the ambulance turned the corner though the light high bell could be heard down the next street and still farther as it crossed the Tottenham Court Road, chiming constantly, it is the privilege of loneliness; in privacy one may do as one chooses.

As Peter stands by the pillar-box opposite the British Museum, there comes to him

> a moment, in which things came together; this ambulance and life and death.

Thus, Peter, like Clarissa, is also related to Septimus in this common attraction to privacy of the soul, life, and death. Theirs is a nonverbal, mystical kind of communication.

Peter's thoughts turn toward Clarissa, and when he reaches his hotel (it is still six o'clock), he finds a letter from her. This further establishes the relation between them, both in thought and in time.

It is the chiming of Big Ben at six o'clock that makes this moment of Septimus's death so dramatic and outstanding. Virginia Woolf refrains from using the clock again as a device until the very end of the book, when the complete relationship between characters and meaning becomes final. When Septimus hurls himself to his death, he becomes one with reality by merging with the stream of life and eternity. He both retains the privacy of soul and becomes a part of the trees, the streets, and the people he has never met.

From this point on, the progression of external time is felt through the activities of the characters and through a poetic description of day fading into night:

> Like a woman who had slipped off her print dress and white apron to array herself in blue and pearls, the day changed, put off stuff, took gauze, changed to evening, and with the same sigh of exhilaration that a woman breathes, tumbling petticoats on the floor, it too shed dust, heat, colour; the traffic thinned; motor cars, tinkling, darting, succeeded the lumber of vans; and here and there among the thick foliage of the squares an intense light hung. I resign, the evening seemed to say, as it paled and faded above the battlements and prominences, moulded, pointed, of hotel, flat, and block of shops,

> I fade, she was beginning, I disappear, but London would have none of it, and rushed her bayonets into the sky, pinioned her, constrained her to partnership in her revelry.

The day disappears into night as Septimus has plunged into death, and as the individual waves fade into the sea; yet life goes on.

The final scene of the book takes place at Clarissa's party where all the important characters who have previously appeared, either in person or in thought, are gathered. The design of the book is completed—all the threads are brought together. Even Septimus makes his appearance, when Lady Bradshaw takes Clarissa aside and tells her about the young man who has killed himself. In this way, the Bradshaws connect the concentric circle of characters whose orbit is Mrs. Dalloway with the concentric circle whose orbit is Septimus,[4] and life and death come together in a unity. When Clarissa hears the news of Septimus's death, she thinks to herself, "Here is death, right in the middle of my party." She remembers how she had once thrown a shilling into the Serpentine but never anything more. She thinks of Peter and Sally Seton who would grow old; but

> this he [Septimus] had preserved. Death was defiance. Death was an attempt to communicate.

Clarissa suddenly feels the terror of life that she had experienced that morning. She walks to her window, and

> in the room opposite the old lady stared straight at her! She was going to bed. . . . [She] pulled

> the blind now. The clock began striking. The young man had killed himself; but she did not pity him; with the clock striking the hour, one, two, three, she did not pity him, with all this going on. There! The old lady had put out her light! The whole house was dark now with this going on, she repeated, and the words came to her, Fear no more the heat of the sun. She must go back to them. But what an extraordinary night! She felt somehow very like him—the young man who had killed himself. She felt glad that he had done it; thrown it away. The clock was striking. The leaden circles dissolved in the air. He made her feel the beauty; made her feel the fun. But she must go back. She must assemble. She must find Sally and Peter. And she came in from the little room.

Big Ben has struck for the last time in the book with the completion of the identification between Clarissa and Septimus. And at the end of the novel, we are very much aware of the present and past merging—Peter and Sally there.

One critic has written of *Mrs. Dalloway* that "Septimus's death is an artistic mistake. . . . Death as defiance, death as a desire to communicate, does not even clarify Mrs. Woolf's idea that death is but an accident in time."[5] How true! And in a novel so artistically executed and flawless, this artistic mistake, as the exception, calls attention to itself—and makes us wonder whether this mistake represents a still unresolved conflict on the part of the author.

In addition, suicide is the one action in the book that adds the dimension of drama and is incompatible with the style of the horizontal novel.

5

TO THE LIGHTHOUSE

Virginia Woolf's next novel continues to show her virtuosity and development. *To the Lighthouse* is an improvement still over *Mrs. Dalloway*. It has more self-contained unity than the latter, largely because of Virginia Woolf's new treatment of psychological and external time.

In *Mrs. Dalloway*, the present lives of the characters are understood in the light of their pasts. Without a knowledge of Bourton, the reader would find Clarissa Dalloway, Peter, Sally, and the others thin indeed, and would not be able to attach much significance to the party that brings them all together again. They are nothing without their pasts, and the book's meaning is dependent upon a period and place outside its own fictional time and setting. Bourton is "an addition to the solid structure"[1] of *Mrs. Dalloway*. *To the Lighthouse*, on the other hand, is completely self-contained within the fictional time span it covers. There is but one major reference to the past which, had it been left out by the author, would have done no damage to the book. William Banks speaks of the Mannings, old friends of Mrs. Ramsay whom she last saw twenty years ago. The present description given by Banks is disappointing to Mrs. Ramsay, and so she refuses to think of them as differently than her perception of them twenty years ago. She is protecting an important memory from time's change and the alteration of events. Without these memories, life to Virginia Woolf would have had no order or meaning.

time's passage—a refusal to recog-
ry to the author's peace of mind.
Woolf does not rely upon a past
recorded in *To the Lighthouse,*
s, upon which the characters look
time covered by the book. While
nsion of one day into a lifetime,
contraction of ten years into one
lealing with more than ten years,
s Mrs. Ramsay's mind by selecting
lifetime, rather than of a day."[3]
is book are divided into three parts
ast part, the characters look back
chapter. The time lived through
tions together add up to less than
es place on a September evening
6:00 P.M. to bedtime, while the
h a morning. It is "Time Passes,"
t describes the ten years hurriedly
ay preserved the memory of the
the last part of the novel preserve
y who has passed away during the
ghthouse is a voyage into the past

lighthouse and Mrs. Ramsay is
hen Mrs. Ramsay, knitting, drifts
l—to a lulling rhythm like that of
s of her inner world. In this con-
t and the range of experience is
peace, and eternity in contrast to

ost the fret, the hurry,
to her lips always some

> exclamation of triumph over life when things came
> together in this peace, this rest, this eternity;
> and pausing there she looked out to meet that
> stroke of the Lighthouse, the long steady stroke,
> for watching them in this mood always at this hour
> one could not help attaching oneself to one thing
> especially of the things one saw; and this thing, the
> long steady stroke, was her stroke.

The lighthouse standing alone in the midst of an infinite ocean symbolizes a moment—a peak of perfection like the Parthenon in *Jacob's Room*—that remains forever free from the ebb and tide of ephemeral life, just as Mrs. Ramsay is a memory that gives meaning to the otherwise fragmentary chaotic lives of the other characters. Mr. Ramsay and his two children, James and Cam, reach the lighthouse at the very moment that Lily Briscoe, an artist, who has begun a painting of Mrs. Ramsay and her son James ten years earlier, puts in the final stroke that completes her picture. The book ends here, a complete picture also, as Lily Briscoe thinks, "I have had my vision." She has recaptured a visual memory of Mrs. Ramsay. Thus, at the end of the novel, a pattern emerges for one instant, and the question Lily poses at the very opening of Chapter III, "What does it mean then, what can it all mean?" is answered.

There is no question as to the perfection of design in this novel. Joan Bennett likens the structure of *To the Lighthouse* to the effect produced by the lighthouse beam—"the long flash represented by the first movement (The Window), the interval of darkness represented by the second movement (Time Passes) and the second and shorter flash by the last movement (The Lighthouse)."[4] "When this aspect of the book is thought of, the subject is no longer a particular group of human beings; it is life and death, joy and pain—more

This is an abnegation of time's passage—a refusal to recognize it—which was necessary to the author's peace of mind.

But although Virginia Woolf does not rely upon a past outside the fictional time recorded in *To the Lighthouse*, there is a past, nevertheless, upon which the characters look back, contained inside the time covered by the book. While *Mrs. Dalloway* is the expansion of one day into a lifetime, *To the Lighthouse* is the contraction of ten years into one day.[2] But we are actually dealing with more than ten years, since Virginia Woolf creates Mrs. Ramsay's mind by selecting "from the experiences of a lifetime, rather than of a day."[3] The ten years covered by this book are divided into three parts of unequal length. In the last part, the characters look back upon the scene of the first chapter. The time lived through in both the first and last sections together add up to less than a day. The first chapter takes place on a September evening lasting from approximately 6:00 P.M. to bedtime, while the last chapter extends through a morning. It is "Time Passes," the intervening chapter, that describes the ten years hurriedly fleeting by. As Mrs. Ramsay preserved the memory of the Mannings, the characters in the last part of the novel preserve the memory of Mrs. Ramsay who has passed away during the ten-year interval. *To the Lighthouse* is a voyage into the past to recapture a memory.

The bond between the lighthouse and Mrs. Ramsay is established in Chapter I when Mrs. Ramsay, knitting, drifts off from the objective world—to a lulling rhythm like that of the sea waves—to the depths of her inner world. In this condition where identity is lost and the range of experience is limited, there is freedom, peace, and eternity in contrast to "suffering, death, the poor."

> Losing personality, one lost the fret, the hurry, the stir; and there rose to her lips always some

> exclamation of triumph over life when things came
> together in this peace, this rest, this eternity;
> and pausing there she looked out to meet that
> stroke of the Lighthouse, the long steady stroke,
> for watching them in this mood always at this hour
> one could not help attaching oneself to one thing
> especially of the things one saw; and this thing, the
> long steady stroke, was her stroke.

The lighthouse standing alone in the midst of an infinite ocean symbolizes a moment—a peak of perfection like the Parthenon in *Jacob's Room*—that remains forever free from the ebb and tide of ephemeral life, just as Mrs. Ramsay is a memory that gives meaning to the otherwise fragmentary chaotic lives of the other characters. Mr. Ramsay and his two children, James and Cam, reach the lighthouse at the very moment that Lily Briscoe, an artist, who has begun a painting of Mrs. Ramsay and her son James ten years earlier, puts in the final stroke that completes her picture. The book ends here, a complete picture also, as Lily Briscoe thinks, "I have had my vision." She has recaptured a visual memory of Mrs. Ramsay. Thus, at the end of the novel, a pattern emerges for one instant, and the question Lily poses at the very opening of Chapter III, "What does it mean then, what can it all mean?" is answered.

There is no question as to the perfection of design in this novel. Joan Bennett likens the structure of *To the Lighthouse* to the effect produced by the lighthouse beam—"the long flash represented by the first movement (The Window), the interval of darkness represented by the second movement (Time Passes) and the second and shorter flash by the last movement (The Lighthouse)."[4] "When this aspect of the book is thought of, the subject is no longer a particular group of human beings; it is life and death, joy and pain—more specifically two themes stand out, the isolation of the individual human spirit and the contrast between the disordered and fragmentary experience of living and the ideal truth or beauty to which the human mind aspires."[5]

To the Lighthouse is the antithesis of *Jacob's Room* in its emotional and structural integration. The opening lines of the book, spoken by Mrs. Ramsay to her son, suggest the journey that will take place the following day:

> 'Yes, of course, if it's fine to-morrow,' said Mrs. Ramsay. 'But you'll have to be up with the lark,' she added.

We are prepared, as we were in *Mrs. Dalloway* for the party that evening, for a point in the future, and not until we return to the past can we actually reach it. There is a merging of past and future in the climactic moments of both books. At the beginning of *To the Lighthouse*, our thoughts dwell upon a point in the future; at the end, they focus upon a point in the past. Of course, the tomorrow that Mrs. Ramsay speaks about to her son does not occur until ten years hence, which expresses Mrs. Woolf's complete objection to the authenticity of external time. It is the thoughts and feelings that count; not until the characters thoroughly understand (though on a subconscious level) the meaning of the lighthouse can they ever attempt to reach it, and this understanding does not come in a day. Reaching the lighthouse is the equivalent of merging with reality. It is a matter of submerging one's individual personality and dipping down into the subconscious—becoming part of a "pool of thought, a deep basin of reality." The climax of the book occurs when the characters all in some way make a tribute to Mrs. Ramsay, who is at one with reality because she is dead. They have made their spiritual journey into reality.

"Time Passes," a poetic description of the ten years gradually setting in upon and changing the empty house left by the Ramsays, occurs immediately following the characters' retirement to bed. It opens with William Banks saying: "Well, we must wait for the future to show"—and closes with Lily Briscoe waking up in the house: "Here she was again, she thought, sitting upright in bed. Awake." The interval of ten years is but a night in the lives of the characters.

During this night many things happen, such as Prue Ramsay's marriage and death in childbirth, Andrew Ramsay's death in an explosion in France, Mr. Carmichael's successful presentation of a volume of his poems, and most important of all, Mrs. Ramsay's death.

> Mr. Ramsay stumbling along a passage stretched his arms out one dark morning, but, Mrs. Ramsay having died rather suddenly the night before, he stretched his arms out, they remained empty.

This picture of Mr. Ramsay with his arms outstretched is symbolic of the emptiness in the lives of all those who knew Mrs. Ramsay (expressed in the beginning of Part III) until they can fill the loss with her memory. These events, or deaths as most of them are, which would play a primary role in an ordinary novel, are spoken of only incidentally by Virginia Woolf. In fact, she encloses the one or two brief statements disclosing this information within parenthesis, as if to show their insignificance. They are but pebbles sinking into an endlessly flowing stream.

The handling of time in *To the Lighthouse* gives the reader the feeling that the present situation of one day (an evening and a morning—Chapter I and Chapter III) is taking place against a background of ten years. Regarding it in wider perspective, it is the temporal against the eternal. What difference does it make how many days or years have passed when we view time in this way! *To the Lighthouse* is but a moment out of eternity, and not the kind of moment that can be measured by our watches. We sense a past, that has no beginning, behind it and a future, that will never end, in front.

This novel does not have to rely upon the artificial methods of *Mrs. Dalloway* to achieve unity. A Big Ben, an airplane in the sky—these are no longer needed to remind us of the hour or to relate characters in space. One reason is that the setting is a small island, a world isolated from the rest of humanity, and the characters are always within close proximity of each other. If one character wishes to see another, he has merely to look up. And instead of a Big Ben to record time, "the flow of time is measured in 'The Window' and 'The Lighthouse' by the natural events of a day—by Mrs. Ramsay's trip to and from the town, by her knitting which she tries to finish before night, by dinner, by bedtime, by the movement of the boat from the bay to the lighthouse, by the newly-caught fish that flop on the bottom of the boat and then lie still—events which are not external to the action, as the striking of Big Ben is, to some extent, external to the action of Mrs. Dalloway."[6]

We must realize that both techniques mentioned in the previous paragraph, are not new to Virginia Woolf, but merely developed. For example, in *A Voyage Out* and the Cornish Beach scene in *Jacob's Room,* she isolates her characters together on an island in order to gain an intensification of personality and establish more closely, without outside interference, their relation to one another. Measuring time by natural events has occurred often in her former works—the emptying of a bag of cherries in *Jacob's Room,* the description of day changing to night in *Mrs. Dalloway,* and so on. And there is a third technique which first appeared in *Jacob's*

Room and, in a modified form, contains the germ of the basic structural idea of *To the Lighthouse:* bringing the past forward to become the present. Jacob meets the Reverend Mr. Floyd for the second time and re-enacts a scene that has already taken place. In *To the Lighthouse* the technique is much more subtle, of course, and logical, with the past returning in the form of a memory.

Although the major reasons for the greater degree of unity in this novel are linked with *time,* there is another, that Johnstone has pointed out, unrelated to time. In *Mrs. Dalloway* the story revolves about two groups of characters, each with a central figure—Clarissa and Septimus. But in *To the Lighthouse* there is only one group of characters, having Mrs. Ramsay as its center.

Virginia Woolf in her persistent use of time and space as the frame for the free-flowing inner consciousnesses of her characters often thought of time and space as inseparable. In Part III of *To the Lighthouse* she writes:

> But what after all is one night? A short space, especially when the darkness dims so soon, and so soon a bird sings, a cock crows, or a faint green quickens, like a turning leaf, in the hollow of the wave.

In this novel, as in her others, the main character of the book is not any person or persons, but rather reality. " 'Life is full of trees and changing leaves' is the book's refrain."[7] Death, although it is not present to the extent that it was in the previous book, is still lurking in the background—and naturally so, since it is part of the author's concept of reality. And, to repeat, although Virginia Woolf succeeds in presenting the inevitable poetically and as something desirable, she still, in certain passages, reveals that her conflict about death continues to be unresolved, as it was in *Mrs. Dalloway:*

> There were the eternal problems: suffering; death; the poor.

Mrs. Ramsay contemplates

> the monotonous fall of the waves on the beach, which for the most part beat a measured and soothing tattoo to her thoughts and seemed consoling to repeat over and over again as she sang with the children the words of some old cradle song, murmured by nature, 'I am guarding you—I am your support,' but at other times suddenly and unexpectedly, especially when her mind raised itself slightly from the task actually at hand, had no such kindly meaning, but like a ghostly role of drums remorselessly beat the measure of life, made one think of the destruction of the island and its engulfment in the sea, and warned her whose day had slipped past in one quick doing after another that it was all ephemeral as a rainbow—this sound which had been obscured and concealed under the other sounds suddenly thundered hollow in her ears and made her look up with an impulse of terror.

You might call this—her best novel—a journey into death as reality.

6

ORLANDO

Virginia Woolf attempts to solve the problem of death in *Orlando* by denying it. Because it has no existence in this novel and is rarely, if ever, referred to except in the most humorous way, we would easily assume that the author had gotten over her death obsession. But before arriving at such a conclusion, let us examine the nature of fantasy, which *Orlando* undeniably is. The primary force behind every fantasy, whimsical and imaginative though it may be, is the wish. What we cannot gain in reality, we possess through fantasy, and Virginia Woolf in *Orlando* possesses eternal youth and life.

In this marvelously whimsical book, Orlando is a lad of sixteen when the story begins in the late sixteenth century and a woman of thirty-six at its conclusion in 1928. Orlando lives for three and one-half centuries. Rather than die, as people ordinarily do, our delightful androgynous character merely drifts off to sleep for a period of days, then awakens with a start to find herself in a new century. On one of these occasions, Orlando opens her eyes to find herself a woman, though formerly a man.

Orlando is many things—a denial of external time and space, a defiance against death, and an analysis of bisexuality. The author enjoys herself immensely as she creates the world just as she would have liked it. Her heroine is a combination of beauty, wit, intelligence, sensitivity, and other admirable features (is wealthy and has position besides) . . . who lives, loves, and meets and surpasses every crisis (except for a betrayal by the beloved one. At the time of the betrayal, however, Orlando is merely an adolescent, and this is to be expected in the biography of every hero or heroine—lending a poignant note to an otherwise successful life).

Despite the book's historical validity, nothing that happens externally is ever treated seriously. Consider, for example, the author's description of England's Great Frost:

> Near London Bridge, where the river had frozen to a depth of some twenty fathoms, a wrecked ferry boat was plainly visible, laying on the bed of the river where it had sunk last autumn, overladen with apples. The old bumboat woman, who was carrying her fruit to market on the Surrey side, sat there in her plaids and farthingdales with her lap full of apples, for all the world as if she were about to serve a customer, though a certain blueness about the lips hinted the truth.

The frivolous tone of this passage is quite consistent throughout the book. Yet beneath her humor and satire, Virginia Woolf is revealing her particular vision of reality which to her was indeed very serious. And there are moments when her question, "What is life?" reaches an almost frantic pitch.

By creating a character who lives for centuries, the author eliminates the need of her previous books, to fill out the present picture with the past. We learn about Orlando's experiences as they occur, and meditation and memory do not have quite the same function as they did in, for instance, the life of Mrs. Dalloway. Yet Orlando meditates profusely—about life, art, fame, and so on—expressing as she does so Virginia Woolf's views on these subjects. And Orlando recaptures moments of her past life through memory, but these are mostly moments that the reader has already witnessed. As always, it is the author's intention in this book to present the workings of a mind. Therefore Virginia Woolf felt compelled to explore memory, which is an important aspect of every consciousness and has a special nature of its own.

Orlando contains a variety of time sequences. There is a past that is referred to but never encountered—Orlando, relating to a maiden his family history, explains that his house was one of the most ancient in Britain, that his ancestors had come from Rome with the Caesars. The time that Virginia Woolf focuses upon primarily in this novel is the three and one-half centuries (1586 to 1928) that Orlando actually lives through. She is giving psychological time an objective reality that it does not possess—but this is fantasy. Fantasy is for Virginia Woolf a way to explore psychological time and substitute it for the clock time that rules our lives. Thus, Orlando is only thirty-six at the conclusion of the book, but she has lived more than three hundred and fifty years. Living can be measured only by experience, not by the artificial units of chronological time. Chronological age is not an indication of real age:

> Indeed, it cannot be denied that the most successful practitioners of the art of life, often unknown people by the way, somehow contrive to synchronize the sixty or seventy different times which beat simultaneously in every normal human system so that when eleven strikes, all the rest chime in unison, and the present is neither a violent disruption nor completely forgotten in the past. Of them we can justly say that they live precisely the sixty-eight or seventy-two years allotted them on the tombstone. Of the rest we

> know to be dead though they walk among us; some are not yet born though they go through the forms of life; others are hundreds of years old though they call themselves thirty-six. The true length of a persons's life, whatever the *Dictionary of National Biography* may say, is always a matter of dispute.

Through Orlando, Virginia Woolf attempts to show some of the "sixty or seventy different times which beat simultaneously in every normal system."

There is an entirely new time dimension that the author introduces in this novel. It is the real time of both reader and author. On page 44 of *Orlando,* Virginia Woolf writes in the midst of a philosophical discussion upon life's mystery

> so that even now (the first of November, 1927) we know not why we go upstairs, or why we come down.

The book ends with a statement of the date:

> . . . and the twelfth stroke of midnight sounded; the twelfth stroke of midnight, Thursday, the eleventh of October, Nineteen hundred and Twenty-Eight.

Slightly less than one year has elapsed from November 1, 1927, to October 11, 1928, in the real time of the reader. Virginia Woolf, in *A Writer's Diary,* mentions *Orlando* for the first time on October 5, 1927, so we can assume that this is when she began writing it. The book was published in 1928. At the end of *Orlando,* the author-reader time merges with Orlando's psychological time; it is October 11, 1928, for all concerned.

Why does Virginia Woolf introduce this author-reader time dimension into her novel? Perhaps because she is writing fantasy and must solidify the relation between herself and the reader for the sake of reality. She, in effect, says to her audience, you and I know that the character Orlando is pure invention, but here are my views on human personality, life, time, and reality—and they are real. Related to this idea is her increased need for an orientation in the present due to the greater freedom she takes with inner psychological time. In addition, *Orlando* is biography, and Virginia Woolf, the biographer, is letting us see Orlando and her times through Orlando's eyes, while, at the same time, is looking back upon Orlando from the twentieth century as a historical figure.

The hero-heroine of this book is based upon Victoria Sackville West, a poet and intimate friend of the author. *Orlando* was meant to reflect both English history and literature from the Elizabethan era to the present together with the environment, behavior, and literary style of Victoria Sackville West. Orlando "changes sex in the course of the book and her environment, behavior and literary style alter as the story progresses to correspond with those aspects of Victoria Sackville West's personal and literary heredity which make her what she was, both biologically and culturally."[1] Thus in the character of Orlando we have not only the biography of a poet but the reflection of three and one-half centuries of English literature and tradition. The sexual change in Orlando from man to woman is an analysis not only of sexual qualities as they appear and become dominant in the development of the human personality but a study of those characteristics that were regarded by the altering standards of society as predominantly masculine or feminine. (This is quite different from *male* and *female* which is not determined by convention.) Orlando is "masculine and violent in the dashing Elizabethan age . . . pensive and morbid in the early seventeenth century

. . . presides at literary tea parties in the Augustan period . . . blushes and swoons in crinolines in the sentimental age of Victoria."[2]

"The Oak Tree," a poem that Orlando invents throughout the course of the biography, is based upon Victoria Sackville West's "The Land" which won the Hawthornden Prize;[3] as this poem develops as a work of art, it reflects the cultural climate of each age in modes of taste and thought. Both Orlando's poem and her house change superficially as the book progresses, but they survive the centuries on the strength of their individuality. They last where human life comes and goes (except, of course, for Orlando, who represents human qualities and the idea of a person rather than a real person) and stand as a tribute to that which is eternal—art. At the end of the book, Orlando draws out her "sea-stained, blood-stained, travel-stained" manuscript of "The Oak Tree":

> She turned back to the first page and read the date, 1586, written in her own boyish hand. She had been working at it for close on three hundred years now. It was time to make an end. Meanwhile she began turning and dipping and reading and skipping and thinking, as she read, how very little she had changed all these years. She had been a gloomy boy, in love with death, as boys are; and then she had been amorous and fluid. And then she had been sprightly and satirical; and sometimes she had tried prose and sometimes she had tried drama. Yet through all these changes she had remained, she reflected, fundamentally the same. She had the same brooding meditative temper, the same love of animals and nature, the same passion for the country and the seasons.

And earlier in the book Virginia Woolf writes:

> . . . things remain much as they are for two or three hundred years or so, except for a little dust and a few cobwebs which one old woman can sweep up in half an hour; a conclusion which one cannot help feeling, might have been reached more quickly by the simple statement that 'Time passed' (here the exact amount could be indicated in brackets) and nothing whatever happened.

The only things that really change at all are determined by unpredictable society and have no real truth anyway; reality, as exemplified in meditation, nature and the seasons, remains forever and ever the same. As for society, we might call this novel an attempt to reveal its absurdity:

> To give a truthful account of London society at that or indeed at any other time, is beyond the powers of the biographer or the historian. Only those who have little need of the truth, and no respect for it—the poets and the novelists—can be trusted to do it, for this is one of the cases where the truth does not exist. Nothing exists. The whole thing is a miasma—a mirage.

Orlando's humor lies in its portrayal of the day's conventions.

In addition to being satire, *Orlando* is also a study of human nature, and along with the various descriptions of Orlando's manners to suit each period is an analysis of Orlando's growth into a many-sided person. The author writes:

> . . . a biography is considered complete if it merely accounts for six or seven selves, whereas a person may well have as many thousand.

Note the relation that this idea has to time:

> For if there are (at a venture) seventy-six different times all ticking in the mind at once, how many different people are there not—Heaven help us— all having lodgement at one time or another in the human spirit.

Orlando was "masculine and violent" in the Elizabethan age but "swooned in crinolines" during the Victorian period. Each of Orlando's selves is related to a definite time, and she is a mixture of all the selves she has ever experienced, the present containing, as it does, all past moments. Memory brings to the present one or more times proceeding simultaneously. Throughout the book and in the little essay on clock time and inner time, we are told that clock time is in no way indicative of mind time. Virginia Woolf rejects completely temporal sequence and continuity. She switches "from one discriminated occasion into the heart of another without warning; seconds expand into years, as when she (Orlando) falls in love and marries in the course of three and one half seconds; years under the oak tree pass like seconds; separate durations telescope and proceed simultaneously. 'Some weeks added a century to his age, others no more than three seconds at most. . . . Life seemed to him of prodigous length. Yet even so, it went like a flash. . . . He would try to think for half an hour—or was it two years and a half?' "[4]

As it has been previously stated, this freedom with inner time required that the author keep her character well orientated in time and place. One method of accomplishing this is inserting within parenthesis such information—often irrelevant to the context of the paragraph but not truly out of place—as the date or season. For example, Orlando stretches out on his elbow silently soliloquizing on a June day. In the next paragraph, while Orlando is still meditating, Virginia Woolf inserts within parenthesis, "it was now winter and very cold." Orlando has just been reminiscing about the past. The sudden shock of the present, which the season and weather in this case connote, brings her suddenly to her feet. This is a favorite trick of the author—to interrupt the random wanderings of the mind with an unexpected poke from the present, such as the chiming of a clock, or any stimulation at all from the immediate environment. Virginia Woolf achieves her transitions in time very naturally, as she did in *To the Lighthouse*, by such devices as the changing of the seasons and landscapes, as well as changes in conventions and manners, and a projection to the outer world of psychological time.

The poetic ending of the book is sober in contrast to its characteristic frivolity. Orlando, wandering through her house, meditates upon life, meaning, and human nature while time takes a predominant position. She reflects that her house no longer belongs to her.

> It belonged to time now; to history; was past the touch and control of the living.

Her house has endured the test of time. Orlando, in a most natural way, drifts back into the past and visually sees it stretched out before her in the long gallery; but the striking of a clock causes her vision to fall to powder. Immediately her face, which had been dark, and all about her become extremely distinct; she regards everything with intense perception, seeing, for example, the separate grains of earth in the flower beds. Orlando is not shattered by the sudden reminder of the present as she had been previously,

> for she was now one and entire, and presented,
> it may be, a larger surface to the shock of time.

Orlando leaves her house and climbs up the path to the flourishing and eternal oak tree. And again the heroine drifts back to the past and Turkey, and again the chiming of a church clock recalls her to the present. But night comes—

> night that she loved of all times, night in which
> the reflections in the dark pool of the mind shine
> more clearly than by day.

And just before midnight there is a great stillness. As the clock strikes twelve, Orlando, in an ecstatic moment, sees the wild goose of poetry; and past and present merge as the book closes on a note of triumph and of pure mysticism.

7

THE WAVES

Virginia Woolf stepped quite naturally from *Orlando* to *The Waves*. Having solved certain artistic and philosophic problems in *Orlando* and having aired her fantasy and gotten it out of her system, so to speak, she was now prepared to sink deeply into the inner life with greater understanding than ever before. To the extent that *Orlando* is a carefree commentary on the inner stream, time, and reality, *The Waves* is a serious, involved exploration into *durée*. So involved is Virginia Woolf that the six men and women she has created are, in reality, different aspects of herself (real and imagined). Furthermore, these characters, in spite of the fact that they are developed as distinct personalities, are, even in the book, parts of the same person; Bernard, one of the six, who sums up their lives at the end of the novel, says that he is the others—Neville, Jinny, Rhoda, Louis, and Susan. Virginia Woolf has not used in the soliloquies a "differentiated style in thought and speech;"[1] each speaks with the same voice. *The Waves* is just as much a biography of one person as Orlando is. Not only does *Orlando* have approximately six selves (accounted for) but also has two sexes; in *The Waves*, there are three men and three women.

Virginia Woolf presents only one aspect of her characters —their inner world, and on a level of the mind that is not completely conscious; we might call this book a study in sensation and mood. Actions and society have been excluded.

And unless the reader is attending carefully, "he may fail to notice some such event as a birth, a marriage, a love alliance, or a death which is referred to in meditation and although submerged beneath the continual flow of life's current, is yet essential to the gradual forming and fixing of personality as well as to the impressions of life created by the whole composition."[2]

To express the nature of the inner stream requires a change in emphasis, for the events referred to in meditation are not casually passed over in real life; *The Waves* exaggerates and makes dominant what *is* passed over in real life.

The technique in presenting the inner world is interior monologue; the author's source of information is herself. It is as if she had discovered different sides of Virginia Woolf (sometimes conflicting) and by great concentration had split each off from the others. By this method of isolation, she could create separate personalities from the distinct parts, while intensifying meanings and catching details that otherwise would have remained hidden. *The Waves* is not merely a book about reality; it is a self-study. And in it, themes of previous books are repeated, deepened, and presented in such a way as to give additional insight into the author, particularly regarding her conflict over death. There are clues to Virginia Woolf's basic reasons for obliterating time and space and merging with *durée*. In fact, she has exposed herself more in this novel than in any of the others. She has taken a bold plunge into her inner being only to rise, in the books that follow, to the surface again and remain there. *The Waves* was the height of her search into psychological reality.

The book has remarkable organic unity; the writing is tightly knit and nothing is wasted. But the structure of this novel is too neat and obvious. Rather than hide it inside the flesh of the novel, the author, with no sense of modesty, has let the skeleton boldly stand out. Virginia Woolf was attempting to show an important relationship between the form and the content; yet, because she calls attention to her technique, there is an artificiality which interferes with the book's message.

In *The Waves*, as in the three previous novels, external time is the frame. The chronological sequence of the progression of a day at the seaside takes place at the same time as the journey from childhood to old age in the innermost thoughts of six characters. A descriptive interlude at the beginning of each chapter paints the atmosphere of the day at a specific time. Then follows the separate interior monologues of the characters in which their time of life corresponds with the hour of day described in the interlude. Virginia Woolf intended the interludes to serve not only as bridges but as the background for the soliloquies. Joan Bennett writes of the descriptive interludes: "Birds, insects, the objects in the house, the quality of light and sound are made to reflect the altering perceptions of man as he passes from youth to maturity. . . . [In the chapter depicting the last stage of adolescence] the complex changes in their personality are symbolized by the behavior of the birds at midmorning . . . the flight and song of the birds have been made to echo the habits of young human beings, uniting into companies, rejoicing in solitude, driven together by fear of a hostile world, competitive yet cooperative, alert yet narrow in vision."[3] Then through the soliloquies of each character we understand their unique reactions, fears, desires, and thoughts. The interludes join their lives with eternal reality.

At the opening of the book, the characters are children; although they have not yet learned to speak, Virginia Woolf presents their impressions as if they were being verbalized; eventually, the interior monologues replace the single sentences. The first interlude describes a sea, indistinguishable from the sky, interrupted by the appearance of the sun and the approach of morning. The children, who were sleeping, awaken; their symbolic birth is synonymous with daybreak. The impressions of life around them are an integral part of the children's thoughts. The book progresses in this manner until its completion. Thus one day at the seashore is inextricably interwoven with a complete human life cycle.

This one day at the seashore is like every other day and recurs infinitely. The sun that appears at morning and fades at night shall always do so; the waves, without termination, shall beat upon the shore. The descriptive interludes describe eternity synonymous with one day. This is the reality—the cyclical recurrence—birth, life, death repeated again and again, day after day. The experience of the present moment, which both lasts forever and is, in Virginia Woolf's words, "transitory, flying, diaphanous" (from *A Writer's Diary*), is juxtaposed against the eternal. Each character is an individual wave that rises from the interminable ocean at birth only to merge once more at death.

The interludes that begin each chapter not only set the stage for a new phase of life—whether it be adolescence, maturity, or old age at an equivalent level with the position of the sun on the horizon—but also interrupt the internal monologues like breaking waves. We pass from one stage of life to another, while the journey of the sun, behavior of the birds, ebb and flow of the waves indicate the passing of time in the temporal lives of the characters. Virginia Woolf presents each stage as a scene—at this moment now. She is a horizontal writer.

In stylized monologues, each character expresses in tight, condensed form his or her particular attitude toward life, which remains consistent throughout. Time's effect upon the individual is to make him know how it feels to be young, middle-aged, or old; its progression does not basically change the person. The experiences of life that time permits merely round out and deepen his childhood attitudes toward the world; there is a repetitive pattern about life. Thus we are able to identify the characters, not by their style of monologue—since this does not vary from person to person—but by the content: the repeated images, desires, and fears, which is "consistent both with the individual and with the time of life."[4] The content is a combination of impressions, meditation, and mood, outside the limits of time and space. Virginia Woolf presents this inner world as though her characters were aware of all that goes on there and are explaining it; yet they could not possibly be conscious of the depth expressed. We know, therefore, that the monologues are not actual speeches but the author's method of revealing both their conscious and unconscious lives.

The soliloquies of the characters run "in and out, in the rhythm of the waves" (*A Writer's Diary*), and the sea images permeate their speeches. It does not take us long to discover the special motivations of each of these personalities and their divergent attitudes toward time and reality. Louis has a strong sense of the past and longs for night and darkness (in Virginia Woolf night and the past are always related). He cannot bear the present—the daytime when he will be laughed at for his "unenviable body," "large nose," "thin lips," and "colonial accent"; and although Virginia Woolf does not write this, we might venture that he cannot stand the isolation and separateness that his feeling of unattractiveness produces. At a school Christmas party, gifts are exchanged, but he is forgotten. It is not surprising that he escapes:

> I am the stalk. My roots go down to the depths of the world, through earth dry with brick and damp with earth, through veins of lead and silver. I am all fibre. All tremors shake me, and the weight of the earth is pressed to my ribs. Up here my eyes are green leaves, unseeing. I am a boy in grey flannels with a belt fastened by a brass snake up here. Down

> there my eyes are the lidless eyes of a stone figure in a desert by the Nile. I see women passing with red pitchers to the river; I see camels swaying and men in turbans. I hear trampling, tremblings, stirrings around me.

And later he says:

> My roots are threads, like fibres in a flower-pot, round and round about the world. I do not wish to come to the top and live in the light of this great clock, yellow-faced, which ticks and ticks.

Yet although Louis fears his individuality and consequent feeling of isolation, he also dreads the loss of it:

> . . . all deaths are one death. . . . Meeting and parting, we assemble different forms, make different patterns. But if I do not nail these impressions to the board and out of the many men in me make one; exist here and now and not in streaks and patches, like scattered snow wreathes on far mountains; and ask Miss Johnson as I pass through the office about the movies and take my cup of tea and accept also my favorite biscuit, then I shall fall like snow and be wasted.

Thus we have another expression of Virginia Woolf's conflict, in her desire for individuality but fear of its loss. The "moments" resolve the conflict because they reflect the eternity where identity is lost, yet stand out separately from the rest of time.

In contrast to Louis is Jinny who lives for the present

moment and the daytime. Darkness, sleep, night, and the future fill her with fright; she cannot stand the thought of death, of aging, of losing her youth and so she obliterates the passing of time by her numerous sexual affairs—needless to say they are brief. She has no past, just a present:

> I cannot follow any word through its changes. I cannot follow any thought from present to past.

Her opposite is Susan who at school longs for home (and the past). Yet Susan who can accept the past, unlike Louis, is comfortable with the present and the future. In her, past and future merge. She is the only character who is at one with reality; she understands, although unconsciously, the meaning of time. At home in the surroundings of nature, she willingly commits herself to the role of mother—the progenitor of the race—and never regrets the passing of time.

> I am the seasons, I think sometimes, January, May, November; the mud, the mist, the dawn. . . . My children will carry me on; their teething, their crying, their going to school and coming back will be like waves of the sea under me.

It is not until the end of the novel that Bernard, as all six of the characters combined, sums up and expresses Virginia Woolf's intellectual conception of time and reality. Since he is the phrase-maker, the would-be writer who observes others, it is quite fitting that he be the author's mouthpiece. Until the end of the novel, he expresses no consistent or distinctive attitude toward time. As a young boy leaving for school, he reveals his characteristic reaction to life in the following statement:

> I must make phrases and phrases and so interpose something hard between myself and the stare of housemaids, the stare of clocks, staring faces, indifferent faces, or I shall cry.

There is in each of the characters, except for Susan, some need to escape from an unbearable reality. With Bernard it is indifferent faces and indifferent clocks. One cannot communicate with indifference, and the result is that one's sense of isolation—of separateness—is increased. The writer can escape through his phrases; he builds bridges and sets up communications between himself and others. But no one can stop the indifferent clocks, which Virginia Woolf tried so desperately to do with her concept of the "moment" wherein time stood still—and personality, ego, and separateness were overcome in a merging with reality.

Neville must escape an old hallucination. Standing on the steps as a child, he overhears through the swing doors the cook telling about the dead man with his throat slit.

> The apple-tree leaves became fixed in the sky; the moon glared; I was unable to lift my foot up the stairs. . . . I shall call this stricture, this rigidity, 'death among the apple trees' forever.

This haunts him all his life and he momentarily escapes this past moment by flights into homosexuality. His first love is Percival, a person who is seen only through the eyes of the six characters. Percival "is a great master of the art of living . . . understands everything . . . and is, so to speak, a centre of reality, a perfectly adjusted person, around whom the six are grouped."[5] And Percival, like the dead man, is associated with swing doors, since he is last seen leaving through one before we learn that he has been flung from a horse in India and killed. "Swing doors appear and reappear throughout the novel, and are always associated with the transitoriness of life."[6] Percival's death, like the childhood memory of the dead man, reinforces the earlier memory and becomes an additional memory that Neville tries to forget but can't. He says to his current love:

> Meanwhile let us abolish the ticking of time's
> clock with one blow. Come closer.

Rhoda is the antithesis of Jinny but bears a relation to Louis. While Louis's mind moves down the stream of time, Rhoda's wanders in space. Virginia Woolf obliterates time and space in the interior monologues of Rhoda and Louis, both of whom dread daytime. Rhoda is a most important character, and it is largely through her that Virginia Woolf reveals herself. A contradiction exists in Rhoda's attitude about life and death that is highly significant if we are to understand the author's mixed feelings about death. For we do not progress far into the book before Rhoda expresses her enormous fear of death. As Rhoda's early childhood comes to an end, she is sinking into sleep but fighting it:

> Let me pull myself out of these waters. But they
> heap themselves on me; they sweep me between
> their great shoulders; I am turned; I am tumbled;
> I am stretched, among these long lights, these
> long waves, these endless paths, with people
> pursuing, pursuing.

She commits suicide later in life (at approximately the same age as Virginia Woolf) and joins the waters that she so strongly resists in childhood. In the passage just quoted, Rhoda expresses a fear of merging with reality and a terror of her own feelings and her unconscious; in Virginia Woolf's writing, *durée* is connected with intuition, loss of personality, the unconscious, sleep, timelessness, the dark, water, and so on. And Rhoda who fears both life and death is helplessly trapped; she can neither accept an identity—"I have no face" (which in Virginia Woolf is related to ego and personality)—nor her own feelings (her unconscious). She is a total stranger both to the world and to herself. She is outside of time and belongs nowhere. In school, unable to solve a mathematical problem, she stares meaninglessly at the blackboard where she has been left alone to find an answer:

> Meaning has gone. The clock ticks. . . . Look, the loop of the figure is beginning to fill with time; it holds the world in it. I begin to draw a figure and the world is looped in it, and I myself am outside the loop; which I now join—so—and seal up, and make entire. The world is entire, and I am outside of it, crying, 'Oh save me, from being blown forever outside the loop of time!'

Louis was not completely outside, since he at least had a past to which he belonged; but Rhoda has neither past nor present nor future. Rhoda as a girl is afraid of sleep, afraid of daytime, yet longs for night:

> There are hours and hours before I can put out the light and lie suspended on my bed above the world, before I can let the day drop down, before I can let my tree grow, quivering in green pavilions above my head.

She cannot sink beneath the waves but must sail above them, on top of them. As Rhoda grows older she sees only silence closing behind her; she has never lived nor become involved in any moment. But a sudden change in her attitude toward death and a loss of fear come through the shock of Percival's death. Like Mrs. Dalloway who identified with Septimus when he threw himself from the window, Rhoda identifies with Percival. She says:

> I will go. I will set aside this afternoon. I will make a pilgrimage. I will go to Greenwich. I will fling myself fearlessly into trams, into omnibuses. As we lurch down Regent Street, and I am flung upon this woman, upon this man, I am not injured, I am not outraged by the collision. A square stands upon an oblong. . . . The structure is visible. We have made a dwelling-place.

So, she at last finds the solution to her problem, and "will at last free the checked, the jerked-back desire to be spent, to be consumed" (*The Waves*). Rhoda goes one step further than Mrs. Dalloway and makes her identification with death complete by flinging herself from the top of the Spanish Hill into the waves below. In Virginia Woolf, death almost always takes the form of a flinging. Even Percival, who is killed, is flung from his horse. The verb is worthy of our attention since it suggests a willed action; and action in Virginia Woolf's writing is practically nonexistent except in the form of death. One might guess that this "action" broke the monotony of pure contemplation or stasis.

Since the structure of the book is so tightly woven with the content, we gain a further insight into the writer by noting not only the descriptive interludes which introduce each chapter and the subsequent time of life, but the endings of each chapter as well. There are nine chapters. The first seven close alternately upon either Rhoda's or Neville's soliloquy. The last two chapters are Bernard's, the interpreter. Let us first examine the alternate speeches of Rhoda and Neville. Together they express an unmistakably negative attitude toward life. Chapter I ends upon Rhoda's fear of herself and of living, Chapter II upon Neville's sense of losing his identity among whirling humanity, Chapter III upon Rhoda's knowledge that she will be "tossed up and down . . . like a cork on a rough sea," Chapter IV upon Neville's announcement that his homosexual love object, Percival, is gone, Chapter V on Rhoda's longing for death—galloping together with Percival into the waves, Chapter VI upon Neville's homosexual affair to escape the present (he is now middle-aged), and Chapter VII on Rhoda envisioning herself climbing to the top of the Spanish Hill from which she will plunge to the waters below. If *The Waves* is supposed to represent the cyclical pattern of reality—birth, life, death, the return of the seasons, and so on, in the introductory passages, the conclusions expressing fear of living, helplessness, loss of love, homosexuality as an escape, death, and suicide do not coincide with the overall purpose of the book—with the exception of death which is a logical ending. However, the deaths that Virginia Woolf has written about are not natural deaths. In spite of herself, Virginia Woolf's true feelings about life force their way out and reveal the basic pessimism that she at times succeeded in hiding through her concept of *durée*. The triumphant moment of peace upon which the book ends—in contrast to this otherwise depressing picture—seems to be the expression of a wish rather than a belief. It was peace, above all, that the author was seeking.

The solution begins in the seventh chapter. Bernard, aware that he has lost his youth, says:

> This drop [of time] falling has nothing to do with losing my youth. This drop falling in time tapering to

> a point. Time, which is a sunny pasture covered with a dancing light, time, which is widespread as a field at midday, becomes pendant. Time tapers to a point. As a drop falls from a glass heavy with some sediment, time falls.

Time is running out; yet soon afterwards he says:

> But let me consider. The drop falls; another stage has been reached. Stage upon stage. And why should there be an end of stages? And where do they lead? To what conclusion?

In Chapter VIII, the six characters meet at Hampton Court, this time without Percival; there is no unity holding them together now that Percival is dead. A silence, in which everything stands still, descends upon them; it is a moment out of time, a moment of reality. And then the ticking of a clock recalls them to the world. Bernard is suddenly filled with an impulse to rise and fight. They prepare to part, saying "it is time," but do not finish their sentences. The chapter ends on Bernard's reflection that life is habit, motion without thought, and it is ebbing away:

> We must go; must catch our train; must walk back to the station—must, must, must. . . . We have been walking for hours it seems. But where? I cannot remember.

In the last chapter Bernard reviews his past along with the lives of the others. This is Virginia Woolf's usual method of bringing forward the past into the present before the climactic moment when past and present meet and form a temporary pattern, a meaning. In recalling the things that happened in the nursery, he says: "All these things happen in one second and last forever." And in a later statement he gives the reason (or at least one of them) for Virginia Woolf's anguish: "We suffered terribly as we became separate bodies."

In Virginia Woolf's great need to deny the ego, the individuality, and merge with the universal oneness of the unconscious, the stream, the waters, death, and timelessness, she is longing for a condition of passivity like that preceding, and immediately following, birth. All her characters are plagued by an inability, in varying degrees, to communicate with one another. Rhoda and Septimus are extreme cases of this.

In *The Waves* the "moments" deal with reunions and separations. In honor of Percival's departure to India, the six characters convene and experience themselves as one unit. The unity is shattered when Percival leaves. And his friends fall to pieces when they learn of Percival's final separation from them through death. They hold a reunion after Percival's death but are without connection. (Note the similarity between this and the disintegration in *To the Lighthouse* after Mrs. Ramsay dies.) Percival is a temporary reality; in death he becomes one with ultimate reality. Bernard enters the National Gallery; Rhoda, a concert hall. "The shock of the news of Percival's death enables both Bernard and Rhoda to step outside the everyday sequence of life for a short time; and art, which is connected with reality, brings each of them closer to Percival."[7] The six characters all are searching for reality—an answer to their individual isolation; and this is completely attainable only in death:

> We strive to make perfect the globe of our lives,
> to reach the Lighthouse, to complete our vision,
> to waste nothing, to be Percival.

Other important moments in their lives are leaving for school, leaving school for work, college, and so on. It is a series of partings until death and then merging with reality.

Bernard continues the theme of Chapter VIII—the progression of routine activities that make up our lives—and adds that underneath this "lie" is

> a rushing stream of broken dreams, nursery rhymes, street cries, half-finished sentences and sights—elm trees, willow trees, gardeners sweeping, women writing—that rise and sink even as we hand a lady down to dinner.

The message in this passage is that under the superficial form and order which we give our lives—the appointments, schedules, and so on—is always our private selves that seem to have no order except for those special moments when harmony is achieved; and this private self, this stream of memories and associations, is forever there, in the background.

In summing up, Bernard uses imagery from the monologues of all the other characters, for they are all parts of him, just as we are all of each other when we become one with the stream:

> Here on my brow is the blow I got when Percival fell. Here on the nape of my neck is the kiss Jinny gave Louis.

He experiences a moment when true meaning is seen, when time stands still, when identity is lost—and Bernard discovers that he no longer has any use for phrases. But once again the outer world of ticking time returns and Bernard summons all his inner forces to confront the enemy—death. (Here again Virginia Woolf expresses a conscious ambivalence toward death.) What Bernard has just experienced is, first of all, meaninglessness, when the pattern imposed upon life by human beings disappears. A pattern is needed but a real one—the sea, the sun, the seasons—not the artificial pattern of routine activities and chronological time. Just before Bernard flings himself against death (the flinging is also toward death demonstrating the conflict between maintaining individuality and surrendering it) as his wave breaks upon the shore, a new dawn has descended upon the world.

> Yes [says Bernard], this is the external renewal, the incessant rise and fall and fall and rise again.

It is not until the end of the book that the reader begins to sense a change in emphasis from that of time running out to time eternal—"the measureless abundance of past time and time to come." Bernard has continued from Chapter VIII the theme of aging, but reverses it:

> It is not age; it is that a drop has fallen; another drop. Time has given the arrangement another shake. Out we creep from the arch of the current leaves, out into a wider world. The true order of things—this is our perpetual illusion—is now apparent.

As in all of her books, the "moment" when a pattern emerges for the split-second, appears at the end. This gives the book finish, makes it a complete expression. And the book itself becomes a "moment"—something that will remain out of the flux and flow of experience.

8

THE YEARS

In this novel emphasis shifts from a study of inner time to that of external time. *The Waves* gives place to *The Years*. The section of *The Waves*—when maturity is reached and the six characters become responsible members of society—is the material for *The Years*, which dwells upon the manners and values of the upper middle class during this period in English history—a span of fifty-nine years, approximating Virginia Woolf's own lifetime.

The author traces the lives of the Pargiter family from 1880 to 1937, the present, choosing random years (1880, 1891, 1907, 1908, 1910, 1911, 1913, 1914, 1917, 1918 and 1937) at which to show the progression from youth to old age that leaves them basically unchanged, as everything comes "over again a little differently." Time ages them and continues on as they ask: "Where am I? Where are we going? Is there a pattern?" A few of the characters, like mystic prophets, perceive a momentary pattern, a glimpse into the other world to which they will be united in death. Their years are spent searching for a meaning, but the meanings they find are only temporary, fragmentary, partial answers—coming in the last chapter—to questions raised throughout the book. Perhaps this was as far as Virginia Woolf could herself go! Young North who is feeling the fragmentariness, the impossibility of breaking through and communicating with others, of knowing himself, is suddenly struck with a new feeling:

> . . . underneath there's the fountain; the sweet nut.
> The fruit, the fountain that's in all of us; . . .

In observing people around him at a party, North, who represents the younger generation, thinks:

> If they want to reform the world . . . why not begin there, at the centre, with themselves?

This is a new realization for Virginia Woolf. She is suggesting that one can look only to himself for his center—not to Percival (*The Waves*), not to Mrs. Ramsay (*To the Lighthouse*). Previously the center was outside, in others. Now union must be with self, a fundamental idea in mysticism. Yet Virginia Woolf did not resolve it in her own life when she joined the external eternal river.

Eleanor Pargiter, whom we first meet as a young woman in *The Years*, now as an elderly lady sums up at the end, as did Bernard in *The Waves*, the meaning of this novel:

> Does everything then come over again a little differently? . . . If so is there a pattern; a theme recurring, like music; half remembered, half foreseen? . . . a gigantic pattern, momentarily perceptible? The thought gave her extreme pleasure that there was a pattern. But who makes it? Who thinks it? Her mind slipped. She could not finish her thought.

When *The Years* ends on the coming of a new dawn, we, the readers, know that that new dawn will never appear in the lifetime of any of the characters. Meaning is only momentary. Both *The Years* and *The Waves* close with the rising of the sun (and *Between the Acts,* the novel to follow, with the rising of a curtain). Virginia Woolf never changed her basic philosophy that each night is followed by day and that this continuum (where death is not an ending) is the meaning of life. The author beckons us to recognize the pattern through construed methods—reappearances of familiar objects that endure the destruction of time (a silver tea caddy, a family portrait), evocations of the past, and juxtapositions of life and death.

Time, the hero of this novel, makes its appearance in the opening paragraph of the book:

> Slowly wheeling, like the rays of the searchlight,
> the days, the weeks, the years passed one after
> another across the sky.

We feel that time is elapsing through the striking of clocks, the years moving on and day fading into night. But when we reach "Present Day" (the last chapter), all clocks cease; we are now living the moment.

Resembling *The Waves,* the introduction of each chapter in *The Years* is a poetic description of the spatial atmosphere —the sun, the wind, the rain. But the descriptions are less universal than they are in *The Waves;* each chapter, headed by the date of that year, gives us a view of London and the countryside and the Pargiter family, who are meant to represent society at that period. And though the author may take a twenty-year hop from one chapter to another, the seasons flow in sequence, expressing the pattern.

By means of scenic arrangements, the author presents several portraits at the same instant. She uses such devices as sparrows echoing a melody of street musicians to unite characters who are spatially separated. These images, which at one level are often rhythms of movement and sound, reflect the pattern of changing seasons at a deeper level and, finally, peace and eternity where there is no movement. She masterfully weaves inner with outer, letting us know what is happening all around a character as well as inside.

The first chapter introduces the members of the Pargiter family while we anticipate the death of the elderly Mrs. Pargiter. When the moment of death finally occurs, it is raining, and Virginia Woolf traces the movement of the rain and its effect upon the still living. The rain takes us to women in childbirth who overhear the doctor saying, "It's raining." The device of the rain is replaced briefly by the tolling of bells at Oxford, not only marking the death of Mrs. Pargiter but introducing the reader to her son Edward who does not know she has died. Death's silence suddenly gives way to the buzz and activity of life. Edward, studying his Greek, reflects:

> But it was no longer silent. He listened; there was no sound in particular; but, as he stood looking out, the building hummed with life. There was a sudden roar of laughter; then the tinkle of a piano; then a nondescript clatter and chatter of china partly; then again the sound of rain falling, and the gutters chuckling and burbling as they sucked up water.

An image from the past interrupts the present. Mrs. Malone, reminiscent of Mrs. Ambrose in *The Voyage Out*, unrolls a strip of embroidery with "a design of birds pecking at fruit copied from a tomb at Ravenna." In the midst of her embroidering (several pages later) she receives a note that Mrs.

Pargiter, her cousin, is dead. Throughout, the clocks chime at chosen intervals to remind the characters of the hour or to enhance a meaningful moment that is timeless. Then at the funeral, Delia, Mrs. Pargiter's daughter is

> possessed by a sense of something everlasting; of life mixing with death, of death becoming life. For as she looked she heard the sparrows chirp quicker and quicker; she heard wheels in the distance sound louder and louder; life came closer and closer. . . .

The chapter ends on the burial in the cemetery.

Although beautifully drawn, the members of the Pargiter family are not that distinguishable as personalities. With few exceptions they are stereotypes of upper middle-class English during the period designated. Virginia Woolf's brilliant perceptions and imagery permit us to see these characters from the outside, but inside they are not individuals; they are all one voice, that of the author. Their lives are a series of meetings and partings. And each time we meet them, they are the same, only older, as they question the meanings of their lives. We hear only incidentally about a marriage, a birth, a death—the events that usually give substance to most people's existence. But Virginia Woolf's characters are uninvolved, unspent, dissatisfied, searching for a moment when time will cease. Action and suspense are absent from the book, except in two rather significant places. The first occurs in Chapter I, where the child Rose Pargiter disobediently steals out on the street one night and is frightened by a sinister-looking man who grabs for her as she hurries by. Later, safe in her room, she seeks solace from her terror by trying to confess to her older sister, Eleanor—but the nurse interrupts. Her experience is buried. She is trapped—like all Virginia Woolf's characters who dare not tell the secret fears and longings of their hearts —and when we meet her again, she is a thirty-nine-year-old spinster, masculine and given to causes.

The second note of suspense also shares this aspect of horror; it is the war (in the chapter "1914") which lends a sense of impending disaster to the characters, but the disaster never truly takes place. However, in the chapter "1917" when air raids drive several people into a cellar, we witness the triumph of brutality and misery over sanity.

Not only does *The Years* lack action but the "moment" itself is experienced by her characters as one of passivity, of quiet contemplation. The characters are also passive in their communications with one another—only saying what is proper, never what is meaningful. No wonder their isolation! North thinks:

> We're all afraid of each other . . . that's what separates us; fear. . . .

His sister Peggy, solitary and unhappy, wants to reach out to North but can't:

> Her hand was still on his arm; she felt something hard and taut beneath the sleeve, and the touch of his flesh, bringing back to her the nearness of human beings and their distance, so that if one meant to help one hurt, yet they depended on each other, produced in her such a tumult of sensation that she could scarcely keep herself from crying out, North! North! North! But I musn't make a fool of myself again, she said to herself.

Eleanor, barely distinguishable as a character from Peggy as a young woman, suddenly changes character when she reaches old age. Originally she is brooding, questioning, and lonely—but magically she becomes flamboyant, extrovertish and highly capable of enjoying the present moment. This stands out as a striking flaw in the book. And I relate it to the false note of optimism at the book's end when we are symbolically presented with the coming of a new dawn. If the days and years to come contain more of the same, they will be dreary.

9

BETWEEN THE ACTS

Virginia Woolf compresses the entire action of this book within a twenty-four-hour day. Time flows effortlessly through the book, and though essential to it and very much in the foreground, never conspicuously so. There is also in *Between the Acts* a sensitive balance in the presentation of inner and outer worlds. The touches seem just right; we see only as much as we should and what we should of the various characters as the author weaves in and out from inner life to objective statement. Virginia Woolf's last book is well executed, sensitively handled, and organically complete. As she put an end to her own disharmonious life, her manuscript was waiting, whole (but not revised), to be sent to the printer as a last contribution to the author's immortality, something that would withstand time's flux and flow.

The heaviness of *The Years* does not carry over into this last novel. But its saner tone still does not eliminate its pessimism. Virginia Woolf's reaction to life and her solution through *action* is illustrated in Giles when he comes upon the following scene:

> There couched in the grass, curled in an olive green ring was a snake. Dead? No, choked with a toad in its mouth. The snake was unable to swallow; the toad was unable to die. A spasm made the ribs contract; blood oozed. It was birth the wrong way round—

> a monstrous inversion. So, raising his foot, he stamped on them. The mass crushed and slithered. The white canvas on his tennis shoes was blood-stained and sticky. But it was action. Action relieved him.

And so Virginia Woolf too put an end to a monstrous inversion, a trap wherein she was both unable "to swallow" (live) or "to die." When she has the character, Mrs. Swithin, say: "Is it time . . . to go and join——" leaving her sentence unfinished, we wonder if Virginia Woolf is completing it in her own mind with "the Ouse River." It is also significant that the title of the book implies an action to take place.

Between the Acts is closest to *Mrs. Dalloway* and *To the Lighthouse* in its structural frame and organic unity. The content is enclosed within the confines of time and space. The time is a June day in 1939; the setting is Pointz Hall and its surrounding estate. Virginia Woolf, having up until this point experimented with time in its structural possibilities, returned to her most satisfactory form. The time dimension and setting are simple, as in *To the Lighthouse*, and the people have no need of clocks to relate them to one another in space, since they are already within visual proximity. The author therefore had an abundance of freedom with which to present the material of her book.

Furthermore, the setting itself gives a sense of past, present, and future merging. Pointz Hall, like Orlando's castle with its centuries of tradition behind it, lends to the book a past and a future; for this house that has lasted these centuries shall exist long after its present inhabitants have died. On the very first page of *Between the Acts* the reader is introduced to an old man seated in an armchair:

> Mr. Oliver, of the Indian Civil Service, retired—said that the site they had chosen for the cesspool

> was, if he had heard aright, on the Roman road. From an aeroplane, he said, you could still see, plainly marked, the scars made by the Britons; by the Romans; by the Elizabethan manor house; and by the plough, when they ploughed the hill to grow wheat in the Napoleonic wars.

The book is a delicately combined texture of different times which exist simultaneously. In addition to the historic and prehistoric past, there is the present and also the future which is implicit in the patterns that keep recurring.

Like Shakespeare's play within a play, the characters watch scenes from a pageant that comment upon their lives. The pageant, presenting scenes of English history, is a traditional ritual of the villagers and takes place annually. It is given on this summer day in 1939, and contains within it all the times covered in the book.

The people who inhabit Pointz Hall eventually become the spectators of the pageant, an event that is inextricably bound up with their lives.

The important characters are old Mr. Oliver whom we have already met, his sister Lucy Swithin, his son Giles, and Giles's wife Isa. In Mrs. Swithin all the time dimensions of the book exist:

> She was given to increasing the bounds of the moment by flights into the past or future; or sidelong down corridors and alleys.

Both she and her brother have memories of their childhood at Pointz Hall and recollections about the old house passed down from their ancestors; their reminiscings bring depth to the present picture. One memory that constantly haunts Mrs. Swithin in a certain room of Pointz Hall is that of her mother rebuking her there. Through Mrs. Swithin's *Outline of History* we delve into the prehistoric past. And there are touches of eternity, too, when she mentions that although she and the others are 150 miles from the sea, "one can hear the waves on a still night." Eternity is present in the house, too, but is felt only in silence—as in the deserted house in *To the Lighthouse*, before the existence of time:

> Empty, empty, empty; silent, silent, silent. The room was a shell, singing of what was before time was; a vase stood in the heart of the house, alabaster, smooth, cold, holding the still, distilled essence of emptiness, silence.

Lucy Swithin and her brother are bound together by "common memories while Isa, mother of the old man's grandchildren, represents the future."[1] Yet Lucy Swithin's thoughts also drift into the future as she looks forward to the pageant and the return of the swallows each year. There is a continuity about it. She has lived long enough to catch glimpses of an emerging pattern among "the scraps, orts, and fragments" that do not add up—a repetition that never ceases. And it is not only her age but her sense of the past that gives her this knowledge. She sees men behaving now as they did in the first stages of life. Yet the complete pattern has not become clear to her; like Isa, she hopes for a meaning—a full answer—that will evolve in the future. Isa, pondering over the isolation engendered by misunderstandings and lack of communication, decides:

> Do we know each other? Not here, not now. But somewhere, this cloud, this crust, this doubt,

> this dust—she waited for a rhyme, it failed her;
> but somewhere surely one sun would shine and all,
> without a doubt, would be clear.

The isolation that surrounds Isa's life is present to greater or lesser degrees in the others also. Mrs. Swithin is partially saved by her profound sense of time; she has a greater feeling of belonging than the others because of this deeper alliance with reality. And despite her scatterbrained nature, she is closer to the truth than any of the others.

Isa, too, has a removed quality about her—a kind of otherworldliness. She is forever roaming along reciting fragments of poetry. She is the melancholic poet who finds beauty both in her sorrow and in a timeless and spaceless world that is attainable only in death—a world where no partings are:

> 'What do I ask? To fly away, from night and day,
> and issue where—not partings are—but eye
> meets eye and. . . .'

Thus Isa wanders because she does not belong; she is "between the acts" of life and death, perhaps, or between two worlds.

> 'Dispersed are we. . . . All is over. The wave has broken.
> Left us stranded, high and dry. Single, separate on
> the shingle. Broken in the three-fold ply . . . now I
> follow' (she pushed her chair back. . . . The man in
> grey was lost in the crowd by the ilex) 'That old
> strumpet' (she invoked Mrs. Manresa's tight, flowered
> figure in front of her) 'to have tea.

She feels stranded and alone. Even marriage and motherhood are meaningless beside her unshared spiritual longings. The unreality of her position is further exemplified in her intense love for a gentleman farmer, "the man in grey," whom she has met but briefly, and pursues entirely in her imagination. She longs for death:

> 'But what wish should I drop into the well?' She looked round. She could not see the man in grey, the gentleman farmer; nor anyone known to her. 'That the waters should cover me,' she added, 'of the wishing well.'

This pageant, which is directed by Miss La Trobe and enacted by the villagers, notes E. M. Forster, presents England's entire history, "into which, at the close, the audience is itself drawn, to continue that history; 'The curtain rose' is its [the book's] concluding phrase."[2] History gradually moves into the present, and the pageant becomes, in a sense, time lived through. It most resembles *Orlando* in this way and also in having a historical background against which the individual lives of the present are juxtaposed. As the pageant is performed, the audience comments upon the scene; the present age reflects upon the past, and the modern world becomes clearer in the light of its past. The spectators comment upon the European situation, and past, present, and future merge.

The distant past is represented in the pageant by cows bellowing in the pastures behind the outdoor stage; these uninvited creatures interrupt the action and we have "the primeval-voice sounding loud in the ear of the present moment." The rain also intrudes upon the scene—a message

all is covered with darkness, and there is a moment of
before the curtain rises at the book's end:

> s night before roads were made, or houses.
> s night that dwellers in caves had watched
> some high place among the rocks.

e continues on this note of hope, and "the cycle of
our hours which the novel describes is merged with
ersal and eternal."[4] But, as in her previous books, the
achieved is temporary; dispersity must again dominate.

from the eternal world. There are other external effects, for example, the tick, tick, tick of the gramophone needle which "seemed to hold them [the audience] together, tranced." Old Oliver's only comment upon this is, "marking time." Time is passing.

We feel that time surrounds and permeates the play. Eternity is expressed in the song of the villagers:

> . . . for the earth is always the same, summer and winter,
> spring; and spring and winter again; ploughing and
> sowing, eating and growing; time passes. . . .

Hints of ancient Greece (the terrace that reminds one of a Greek temple, the mention of Agamemnon and of Clytemnestra, and the villagers in the role of Greek chorus) recall a past that begins before the action of the play.

"Between the acts" of the play, the audience disperses and we delve into their inner lives, as "each turns to his own role."[3] The theme of the pageant and of the book is unity/dispersity, resounding from the gramophone. There is unity when the audience's attention is focused upon the play, when there is a common center of attention, a completeness, a "moment"; but dispersity ensues "between the acts" when everyone is left to feel his individual isolation. The integration during the play results from the merging of times—past, present, and future.

Miss La Trobe typifies the unhappy artist who attempts to create out of the chaos and disorder of life a pattern. She is in ecstasy when her vision is complete and there is unity, in agony when the audience's attention is lost and the crowd disperses.

The last act is ten minutes of present time. The scene is

the rebuilding of an incomplete wall by a man with a hod and a woman handing him bricks. Children, symbolizing the future generation, hold a cracked mirror and flash hand glasses in front of the audience, as a voice asks them to consider themselves; but they try to shade from their eyes the "scraps, orts and fragments" that the mirrors reflect. The last scene is a brutal comment upon man's condition and the impending World War II. The repetitious "ding, dong, ding" of the machine throughout the pageant is an ominous sound that brings to mind a passage from *A Writer's Diary* written on August 28, 1938:

> Ding dong bell . . . ding dong—why did we settle in a village? And how deliberately we are digging ourselves in! And at any moment the guns may go off and explode us. L. [Leonard Woolf] is very black. Hitler has his hounds only very lightly held. A single step—in Czechoslovakia—like the Austrian Archduke in 1914—and again it's 1914. Ding dong ding dong.

There is an almost insane helplessness in these words.

Unity and dispersity are embodied in the two opposing emotions, love and hate. Hate perhaps is what keeps us all apart. As Isa watches the play, she thinks:

> Did the plot matter? She shifted and looked over her right shoulder. The plot was only there to beget emotion. There were only two emotions: love and hate. There was no need to puzzle out the plot.

Then, as the beldame in the pl
and is pronounced dead, Isa sud

> Peace was the third emotion.
> Three emotions made the pl

And we know by now that it was
able only during a "moment" wl
trated, or in death—that the autl
for.

At the end of the play, on the
villagers and guests leave the sc
remains. Mrs. Swithin returns to h
reflects upon the prehistoric past
alone together for the first time tha
ascends the staircase to bed, she re

> Prehistoric man . . . half-humar
> himself from his semi-crouching
> great stones.

Isa and Giles, now alone together, ex
unity:

> Before they slept, they must fight
> fought, they would embrace. Fron
> another life might be born. But
> fight, as the dog fox fights with the
> heart of darkness, in the fields of

Pointz H
eternity

> It w
> It w
> from

Thus li
twenty-f
the univ
pattern

10

CONCLUSION

Until now my conclusions about the author have been drawn from her writings. There is, however, biographical material that further illuminates the picture and substantiates already founded opinions. For one, Virginia Woolf's love of literature and history was greatly influenced by her father's library with its voluminous collection of books covering every period in history. Virginia Woolf, a voracious reader, had unlimited access to it. It is more than likely that she entered into a timeless world—where past and present merged—when she stepped into her father's library.

Then in her teens and early twenties, following the deaths of her mother and father, she had attacks of "melancholia" (and avoided its recurrence, so she wrote in her suicide note, when she took her life in 1941). During this sickness, she lost her time sense. This we learn from an essay that she wrote upon being ill. Her descriptions of what time seemed to her then can be compared to the frequent occasions in her novels when she wanders freely through time and space.

But her preoccupations with time as Aileen Pippett's biography points out was also quite natural, living in London as she did at the turn of the century. London, says Miss Pippett, was a "city of innumerable churches, almost all of them equipped with peals of bells and chiming clocks. Big Ben had hundreds of competitors in announcing the time every quarter of an hour. . . . Little wonder that Virginia's thoughts so often turned to time, since she was so constantly reminded of its passage."

The moset telling bit of information about Virginia Woolf's life comes from her recent biography by Quentin Bell. He discloses the fact of Virginia Woolf's sexual molestations by her older stepbrother when she was a child (which she felt, so the book claims, spoiled her life before it had begun). The similarity between these sexual encounters and the frightening night of the child Rose in *The Years* is more than poetic invention. The experiences must have left Virginia Woolf with a permanent terror and contributed, I believe, to her feeling of separation. Since she could tell none of her family of her victimizations nor understand the feelings they roused in her, she had no recourse but to bury them deep inside, which resulted in separation from a part of herself. It is possible that she attempted to rejoin this separated self in mysticism. This plus her need to be reunited with those loved ones who had been separated from her by death resulted in a desperate wish for unity.

In *To the Lighthouse*, Lily Briscoe struggles toward unity with Mrs. Ramsay, a remote figure who, to her, represents life's significance. But Mrs. Ramsay is unattainable, something that all of Virginia Woolf's chief characters strive for but can never achieve. Unity between Mrs. Ramsay and Lily is finally accomplished, however, only when the deceased Mrs. Ramsay returns in the form of a memory to the artist who captures her forever on canvas. This is the closest she is permitted to approach Mrs. Ramsay and life's meaning. In similar manner, the six characters of *The Waves* grope for the reality embodied in the figure of Percival. Percival is to the reader merely a name; his essence is never demonsrated, merely alluded to. When he is killed, life's meaning disappears for all of the characters but Rhoda, who at last finds a solution to her emptiness and misery by reuniting with Percival in an act of suicide. And then there is Mrs. Dalloway who seeks haven from the exterior world of people and events by reflecting upon an old lady in the room opposite her window. At the end of the book, thinking about the suicide of the young man she doesn't even know, she retreats from the party to watch the old lady put out the light; there suddenly comes to her a great surge of joy as she worships death and the privacy of the soul.

It would appear that Virginia Woolf herself (if we listen to the characters who speak her mind) was tormented by an inability to ever overcome the boundaries of self and unite with another human being. The detached artist in *To the Lighthouse* suffers an agonizing frustration because she cannot penetrate "the soul" of Mrs. Ramsay. Percival exists in *The Waves* not as a flesh-and-blood human being, but as an allusion. This makes unity with the nonexistent man an impossibility, and life's meaning, which is to be found in him, has no reality. Clarissa Dalloway experiences an identification with a dead man whom she does not know, because he has willfully ended his life. If unity was not possible in life, then what remains but death!

So much of her writing reflects the dissatisfaction Virginia Woolf felt. Eleanor in *The Years* ponders:

> There must be another life. . . . Not in dreams, but here and now, in this room, with living people. . . . This is too short, too broken. We know nothing, even about ourselves.

Maggie says:

> Am I that, or am I this? Are we one, or are we separate. . . .

Peggy questions:

> But how can one be "happy" in a world bursting with misery. On every placard at every street corner was Death; or worse—tyranny, brutality, torture; the fall of civilization; the end of freedom.

Characters constantly observe the lives of others who seem to be living, dancing, talking, and so on—as if they themselves are strangers, uninvolved; as if life is outside them while they think about death. We hear the clocks incessantly ticking, feeling the emptiness within the ticking. Life was often like that to Virginia Woolf. It was her pain behind the emptiness, the fragmentariness, the meaningless conversations where no one says what he means. Her suicide, I believe, was not only to avoid mental illness but to overcome her sense of isolation and regain unity in death.

In the unattainable characters such as Mrs. Ramsay there echoes the memory of Virginia Woolf's mother, who died when the author was only thirteen. Her mother died suddenly, as did Mrs. Ramsay in *To the Lighthouse* (as did Rachel, and Jacob, who was based upon Virginia Woolf's brother Thoby). Aileen Pippett in her biography of Virginia Woolf comments on the effect of this death upon the author: "Virginia was never able to describe, to admit, or to recover from this shattering blow. She tried and tried and tried; every known device, to numb the pain, avert the horror. All to no avail. She tried illness and madness, retreating into that dream world where there is no death, the glorious, terrible, unimaginable world where one is completely united with Love itself, beyond the possibility of fear and pain and anguish, never again to be forsaken and alone. . . . When health and sanity returned Virginia was, she thought, secure behind the defense she had automatically erected in the very moment of anguish. No, she did not really feel anything."[2]

Her pain, however, helped open the door to her mysticism, tuned her in to a deeper reality. Though one may argue that this reality exists, night *does* follow day, the seasons *do* change, art *does* endure, and man can feel centered in a world of chaos and confusion. There are moments when reality is penetrated.

It was Virginia Woolf's special privilege to spontaneously enjoy a state of mind that people interested in consciousness strive for through contrived methods. Was hers a gift? Or was it perhaps a result of her intense sensitivity and perception? Did it stem from her desperate need to overcome isolation and be one with a greater outer force? Did her illness contribute? These are questions for speculation.

But her vision was true for her. And in her writing she created her own pattern—drawing order out of chaos. Her work stands as an achievement of the immortality she so passionately sought. She reached her lighthouse.

When she entered the timelessness of the Ouse River, she left behind memories to those who knew her, and her writings to endure forever. These will remain, as the Parthenon remains, monuments of mankind's striving toward perfection and beauty in an imperfect world. Writing was her way to overcome the fragmentariness and the feelings of separateness that so agonized her. Her work was her "moment." It was an action against hopeless surrender and passivity. And finally she accepted suicide as a defiance against the outrage.

NOTES

CHAPTER 1

1. A. L. Mendilow, *Time and the Novel,* p. 149.
2. B. R. Redman, *Saturday Review of Literature,* p. 18.
3. Mendilow, *op. cit.,* p. 150.
4. Robert Humphrey, *Stream of Consciousness in the Modern Novel,* p. 49.

CHAPTER 2

1. David Daiches, *Virginia Woolf,* p. 29.
2. *Ibid.,* p. 22.
3. J. K. Johnstone, *The Bloomsbury Group,* pp. 325-26.
4. Daiches, *op. cit.,* p. 29.

CHAPTER 3

1. Clive Bell, "Virginia Woolf," *Dial,* p. 463.
2. Daiches, *op. cit.,* p. 59.
3. Johnstone, *op. cit.,* p. 331.
4. *Ibid.*
5. *Ibid.*
6. Bernard Blackstone, *Virginia Woolf: A Commentary,* pp. 67-68.

CHAPTER 4

1. John Hawley Roberts, " 'Vision and Design' in Virginia Woolf," *PMLA* (from Roger Fry's *Vision and Design*, pp. 71-75).
2. Elizabeth Bowen, "Time, Period, and Reality," *The Listener*, p. 752.
3. Blackstone, *op. cit.*, p. 10
4. Bennett, *op. cit.*, pp. 113-14.
5. N. E. Monroe, *The Novel and Society*, p. 206.

CHAPTER 5

1. Johnstone, *op. cit.*, p. 347.
2. *Ibid.*, p. 346.
3. *Ibid.*, p. 349.
4. Bennett, *op. cit.*, p. 118.
5. Humphrey, *op. cit.*, p. 101.
6. Johnstone, *op. cit.*, p. 349.
7. Blackstone, *op. cit.*, p. 28.

CHAPTER 6

1. Daiches, *op. cit.*, p. 93.
2. Blackstone, *op. cit.*, p. 131.
3. Winifred Holtby, *Virginia Woolf*, pp. 165-66.
4. Mendilow, *op. cit.*, pp. 228-29 (inner quote is Chapter II, pp. 58-59, *Orlando*).

CHAPTER 7

1. Bennett, *op. cit.*, p. 39.
2. *Ibid.*, p. 123.

3. *Ibid.*, pp. 120-21
4. *Ibid.*, p. 39.
5. Johnstone, *op. cit.*, p. 359.
6. *Ibid.*, p. 365.
7. *Ibid.*, pp. 365-66.

CHAPTER 9

1. Bennett, *op. cit.*, p. 137.
2. E. M. Forster, *Virginia Woolf*, p. 18.
3. Daiches, *op. cit.*, p. 117.
4. Johnstone, *op. cit.*, p. 371.

CHAPTER 10

1. Aileen Pippett, *The Moth and the Star*, p. 47.
2. *Ibid.*, pp. 20-21.

BIBLIOGRAPHY

PRIMARY

The Voyage Out. London: The Hogarth Press, 1949 (first published 1915).

Night and Day. London: The Hogarth Press, 1930 (first published 1919).

Jacob's Room. New York: Harcourt, Brace and Company, 1923 (first published 1922).

Mrs. Dalloway. New York: Harcourt, Brace and Company, 1925.

To the Lighthouse. London: Everyman's Library, 1952 (first published 1927).

Orlando, A Biography. New York: Penguin Books, Inc., 1946 (first published 1928).

"The Sun and the Fish," *The New Republic* (February 8, 1928), pp. 321-23.

"A New Dress," *Significant Contemporary Stories.* Edited by Edith Mirrielees. New York: Double Day, Doran and Company, Inc., 1929.

The Waves. New York: Harcourt, Brace and Company, 1931.

Flush, A Biography. New York: Harcourt, Brace and Company, 1933.

The Years. New York: Harcourt, Brace and Company, 1937.

Between the Acts. Baltimore: Penguin Books, 1953 (first published 1941).

A Writer's Diary (extract from the diary of Virginia Woolf). Edited by Leonard Woolf. London: Hogarth Press, 1953.

SECONDARY

Books

Beach, Joseph Warren. *The Twentieth Century Novel, Studies in Technique*. New York: Appleton-Century-Crofts Inc., 1932.

Bell, Quentin. *Virginia Woolf, A Biography*. New York: Harcourt Brace Jovanovich, 1972.

Bennett, Joan. *Virginia Woolf and Her Art as a Novelist*. New York: Harcourt, Brace and Company, 1945.

Blackstone, Bernard. *Virginia Woolf: A Commentary*. New York: Harcourt, Brace and Company, 1949.

Brewster, Dorothy. *Virginia Woolf*. New York: New York University Press, 1962.

Chambers, R. L. *The Novels of Virginia Woolf*. London: Oliver and Boyd, 1947.

Collins, A. S., Ph.D. *English Literature of the Twentieth Century*. London: University Tutorial Press, 1951.

Daiches, David. *The Novel and the Modern World*. Chicago: The University of Chicago Press, 1939.

———. *Virginia Woolf*. Editions Poetry London, 1945.

Edel, Leon. *The Psychological Novel*. Baltimore: Lippincott, 1956.

Forster, E. M. *Virginia Woolf*. New York: Harcourt, Brace and Company, 1942.

Freedman, Ralph. *The Lyrical Novel: Studies in Hermann Hesse, André Gide and Virginia Woolf*. New Jersey: Princeton University Press, 1963.

Hoare, Dorothy M. *Some Studies in the Modern Novel*. Connecticut: The Prospect Press, 1940.

Holtby, Winifred. *Virginia Woolf*. London: Wishart and Company, 1932.

Humphrey, Robert. *Stream of Consciousness in the Modern Novel*. Berkeley and Los Angeles: University of California Press, 1954.

Johnstone, J. K. *The Bloomsbury Group*. New York: The Noonday Press, 1954.

Kelley, Alice Van Buren. *The Novels of Virginia Woolf: Fact and Vision*. Chicago: University of Chicago Press, 1973.

Krey, Laura. "Time and the Novel," *Twentieth Century English*. Edited by William S. Knickerbocker. New York: Philosophical Library, Inc., 1946.

Mendilow, A. L. *Time and the Novel*. New York: Peter Nevill, 1952.

Moody, Anthony David. *Virginia Woolf*. New York: Grove Press, 1963.

Monroe, N. Elizabeth. *The Novel and Society*. Chapel Hill: University of North Carolina Press, 1941.

Muir, Edwin. *The Structure of the Novel*. London: The Hogarth Press, 1949 (first impression, 1928).

Nathan, Monique. *Virginia Woolf*. New York: Grove Press, 1961.

Pippett, Aileen. *The Moth and the Star, A Biography of Virginia Woolf*. Boston: Little, Brown and Company, 1953.

Richter, Harvena. *Virginia Woolf: The Inward* Voyage. New Jersey: Princeton University Press, 1970.

Tindall, William York. *Forces in Modern British Literature 1885-1946*. New York: Alfred A. Knopf, 1947.

Vogler, Thomas A., ed. *Twentieth Century Interpretations of To the Lighthouse: A Collection of Critical Essays*. New Jersey: Prentice Hall, 1970.

Articles

Allen, Agnes. "Still a Man's World." *Saturday Review of Literature* (August 27, 1938), p. 4.

"An Artist Vanishes." *Time* 37 (April 14, 1941), pp. 34-35.

Bell, Clive. "Virginia Woolf." *Dial* 77 (December, 1924), pp. 451-65.

Bowen, Elizabeth. "Time, Period, and Reality." *The Listener* LVI No. 1441 (November 8, 1956), pp. 751-52.

Burra, Peter. "Virginia Woolf." *19th Century* 115 (January, 1934), pp. 112-25.

Daiches, David. "Virginia Woolf." *Time* (Review) 40 (August 17, 1942), pp. 78-80.

Forster, E. M. "The Novels of Virginia Woolf." *The Yale Review* ns 15 (April, 1926), pp. 505-14.

"How Time Passes." *Time* 29 (April 12, 1937), pp. 93-96.

Jones, H. M. "Two Posthumous Novels." *Saturday Review of Literature* (Review of Between the Acts), (October 25, 1941), p. 7.

Josephson, Matthew. "Virginia Woolf and the Modern Novel." *The New Republic* (April 15, 1931), pp. 239-41.

"Meteorites." *Time* 43 (April 24, 1944), p. 102.

Muir, Edwin. "Virginia Woolf." *The Nation* 122 (June 30, 1926), pp. 721-23.

Muller, Herbert, J. "Virginia Woolf and Feminine Fiction." *Saturday Review of Literature* (February 6, 1937), pp. 3-14.

Redman, Ben Ray. "Incomplete Mystic." *Saturday Review of Literature* (July 23, 1949), p. 18.

———. "Virginia Woolf's Last Comments." *Saturday Review of Literature* (June 17, 1950), pp. 16-17.

Roberts, R. Ellis. "A Biographer Manquée." *Saturday Review of Literature* (October 3, 1942), pp. 25-29.

———. "Virginia Woolf: 1882-1941." *Saturday Review of Literature* (April 12, 1941), p. 12.

Roberts, John Hawley. "'Vision and Design' in Virginia Woolf." *PMLA* 61 (1946), pp. 835-47.

Spencer, T. "Mrs. Woolf's Novels." *New Republic* 113 (December 3, 1945), p. 758.

"Suicide Note." *Time* 37 (May 5, 1941), p. 97.

Wilson, James S. "Time and Virginia Woolf." *Virginia Quarterly Review* 18 No. 2 (April, 1942).